MOZART

Unfinished portrait of Mozart by Josef Lange, painted about
1782

MOZART

BY

CHARLOTTE HALDANE

GREENWOOD PRESS, PUBLISHERS
WESTPORT, CONNECTICUT

Library of Congress Cataloging in Publication Data

Haldane, Charlotte Franken, 1894-1969.
   Mozart.

   Reprint of the ed. published by Oxford University
Press, London.
   Includes index.
   1. Mozart, Johann Chrysostom Wolfgang Amadeus,
1756-1791.
ML410.M9H15 1976   780'.92'4 [B]   75-3733
ISBN 0-8371-8062-7

© Oxford University Press 1960

Originally published in 1960 by Oxford University Press, London,
New York

This reprint has been authorized by the Oxford University Press

Reprinted from copy in the collections of the Brooklyn Public Library.

Reprinted in 1976 by Greenwood Press,
a division of Williamhouse-Regency Inc.

Library of Congress Catalog Card Number 75-3733

ISBN 0-8371-8062-7

Printed in the United States of America

TO

JOHN COWAN

CONTENTS

ILLUSTRATIONS

ACKNOWLEDGEMENTS

The Author wishes to express her gratitude to Miss Emily Anderson and Macmillan & Co. for permission to include many extracts from her admirable translation of *The Letters of Mozart and his Family*; to Robert Keys for the loan of the English translation of the original libretto of *The Magic Flute*; and to the staffs of the Central Music Library and Kensington Borough Council Library for much kind assistance in research.

PART ONE: CHILDHOOD

Chapter I

INFANT PRODIGY

JOANNES CHRYSOSTOMUS WOLFGANGUS THEOPHILUS MOZART was born on 27 January 1756 at Salzburg, Austria. He was the last child of Leopold and Anna Maria Mozart, née Pertlin.

Leopold Mozart is usually remembered only as the father of his famous son. Nevertheless he was a considerable character in his own right. He was a Bavarian, born in Augsburg in 1719. His own father was a prosperous bookbinder, so that Leopold came of the higher artisan class, and received a good education. The family were pious Catholics and Leopold's godfather had him trained as a choir-boy and church organist, with a view to his entering the priesthood.

When Leopold's father died he was sent to the University of Salzburg. There he discovered that he had no priestly vocation and studied philosophy and law. But he was a competent musician, and in 1743 entered the service of the Archbishop of Salzburg, Sigismund von Schrattenbach. It was a great and powerful archbishopric and this prince of the Church kept up considerable state. Apart from the ecclesiastical music there was a court orchestra to provide secular entertainment. Leopold was appointed assistant conductor to this band; he also composed, but concentrated in particular on studying and later teaching the violin. In June 1756, six months after Wolfgang's birth, his father published his *School of Violin Playing* ('Violinschule'), a textbook which brought him lasting distinction in professional musical circles.

Leopold Mozart took himself and his world very seriously indeed. He was a typical South German in that he was methodical and thorough, shrewd and business-like, carefully planning each of his moves well in advance. And he needed to do so, for he lived in a rude and dangerous age, in a small-town atmosphere of intrigue and malice, where a man who wished to succeed in life had to watch his step and also his tongue.

He was a thin, tough little man, not at all given to unruly manners or to easy laughter. Yet he had a dry if rather didactic kind of humour, was a keen observer of men and events, and could express himself with remarkable and occasionally picturesque fluency, so that his letters are even today unusually entertaining to read. But his character lacked grace. He had neither the easy-going manner of the average South German nor the Austrian charm and gaiety. His outlook definitely inclined to pessimism.

Leopold had a very poor opinion of most of his fellow-men, and especially of all artists (with a few rare exceptions) and professional musicians, whom he regarded as ignorant, bad-mannered, and generally drunken varlets:

> Mark well, my son, that *to find one man in a thousand*, who is your true friend from unselfish motives, is to find *one of the greatest wonders of this world.*
>
> On our first visit (to Paris) . . . I avoided all acquaintances, and, mark you, particularly *all familiarity with people of our own profession* . . .
>
> I shall say nothing about women, for where they are concerned the greatest prudence and reserve are necessary, Nature herself being our enemy . . .

His letters to his son in later years were full of such dogmatic assertions, admonitions and warnings.

Perhaps it was partly due to this acidity in his character that although Leopold spent his whole life in service to the archbishopric he never rose to a very high position.

Until the birth of Wolfgang, however, he found consolation and compensation in two main supports—religion and matrimony. His piety was deep and genuine and from their earliest years he gave his children a strictly religious upbringing.

His wife, Anna Maria Pertlin, was born at St Gilgen on the Wolfgang Lake. They were married in 1744. She was an orphan and wholly and completely devoted to her husband and children. From her letters to her husband it is clear that she was a merry soul, with a keen appreciation of the simpler pleasures, such as good food and wines, pleasant company, nice clothes and fashion. Her husband must have seemed a very learned man to her, for in addition to music, which was his profession, Leopold was interested in everything, from politics to painting. Anna Maria Mozart was not a lady, a term that in the eighteenth century meant strictly a feminine member of the aristocracy or landed gentry, but neither was she a woman of the people or a peasant girl. In her day young girls were frequently illiterate or almost so. She had, however, learned to read and write, presumably at her convent, although even in later years her syntax and spelling were still somewhat erratic. Her letters to her husband also occasionally contained certain crude expressions, which in those days, presumably, were not considered in the least shocking. For the rest she was a perfect wife, a devoted mother, cheerful, affectionate, and a little fatalistic, with a firm, although unfortunately not always justified belief that everything would come out all right in the end.

Mozart's parents had seven children, of whom only two survived: the fourth, a girl, Maria Anna generally called Marianne or Nannerl for short, born on 30 June 1751, and Wolfgang, born nearly five years later. Marianne was a bright and also very musical child and was soon being taught to play the harpsichord and clavichord by her father.

Wolfgang was a mere toddler when, before he was three, he began to pick out chords—thirds—on these instruments, showing intense pleasure as he did so. When Nannerl was seven, her father compiled a small collection of pieces for her to practise. The little boy was barely four when his father began to teach him, also, a few simple minuets and other pieces. He would take half an hour to memorize a short one, an hour if it were longer, and would then play them perfectly. By the time he was five he had begun to compose little pieces of his own, which Leopold wrote down for him.

And so it happened that to their astounded delight Wolfgang's parents discovered when he was not yet six years old that he showed every sign of the most precocious and fantastic musical genius. In 1762 Leopold began another little music-book for Wolfgang. His earliest compositions have thus very fortunately been preserved.

Even before Mozart's day there had been Handel to prove that great musical talent can, and generally does, appear in very early youth, in which it seems to differ from other artistic and creative abilities. But a mathematical gift also seems sometimes to show itself very early, although not in a directly creative sense. This was so in Mozart's case. In his delight at discovering figures as well as notes, Wolfgang used to chalk sums over all the available walls and furniture in his home and even on the staircase. In his early years there was never any distinction for him between work and play; his work was music, but music was also his chief recreation and delight. He never went to school. His father was his only schoolmaster and taught him Latin and German as well as music and arithmetic. And he was a stern as well as loving teacher.

As soon as Leopold realized that he had sired a genius his whole outlook on life altered. In sincere piety he honestly believed that God had entrusted this child to him with the command henceforth to devote his own career to him. His personal ambitions were put aside; until Wolfgang was twenty-five years old he was under his father's tutelage, his predominant responsibility, the very core and centre of both his pride and his anxiety.

As a small child Wolfgang's gifts were already so remarkable that Leopold decided that his son could not remain cooped up in a small provincial town such as Salzburg. The whole world lay open to him and he must set forth to conquer it, beginning his triumphal tours at the greatest Courts in Europe. So, carefully, with his usual methodical approach to any problem, Leopold began to organize that conquest. He has been reproached by some of Mozart's biographers for having forced the boy on too early and set him on the path of a professional performer long before the child himself was ready to face the strain of such a career. But it is difficult to see what else his father could have done unless he had been willing to allow him to bloom unseen and especially unheard in Salzburg. Nearly all gifted children love showing off. Wolfgang was certainly always willing to do so. One of his most striking characteristics was the fact that from earliest childhood he himself never had the slightest doubts of his own genius. All children, too, love praise and presents and these he received in almost overwhelming measure as soon as he appeared in public. Although he never had any childhood companions except his sister, he does not seem to have missed them at all. With musical adults he had not a trace of timidity, but fascinated them by talking to them as a mature colleague might have done, whilst remaining in every other respect a gay, mischievous, happy little boy.

The term 'infant prodigy' implies exceptional precocity. All the evidence about Mozart's early years confirms that he was amazingly advanced at every age. His portraits also prove this, for in all of them he looked older than he actually was. His incredibly early maturity as a performer was also accompanied by an utter lack of shyness or self-consciousness, either in private or in public. Yet—and this trait remained one of his most marked characteristics throughout his life—he could not bear to play to any but genuinely musical listeners. At the slightest lack of attention or interruption to the music he would, as a child, sometimes burst into tears, and, both in his earliest years and later, on such distressing occasions he would immediately stop playing and refuse implacably to continue.

Wolfgang fully returned his father's devotion. Leopold was to remind him many years later, as much in sorrow as in anger, how as a child 'when in the past I used always to guess aright and often foresee the future, you used to say in fun: "*Next to God comes Papa*".'

The blend of childishness and precocity in Wolferl—his pet name—is illustrated by a story told by one of Leopold's friends and colleagues.[1] When his father came home from church with him, they found Wolfgang, pen in hand:

'What are you doing?' his father asked him.
Wolfgang: 'A piano concerto. The first part is nearly finished.'
His father: 'Let's look at it. It must be something good.'
Wolfgang: 'No, it isn't finished yet.'

His father took it from him and showed his friend a scribble of notes which were barely legible, as they had mostly been written down over ink-blots which he had mopped up: for the child had been dipping his pen right down to the bottom of the ink-well and each time a drop had fallen from it, he had merely brushed it away with the flat of his hand, continuing to write over it. At first both friends laughed at this conglomeration of notes. But when his father had studied the actual composition carefully, he stared for a long time at the paper, until bright

---

[1] Quoted from Erich Valentin in *Der früheste Mozart*.

tears, tears of admiration and joy, filled his eyes. 'See, my friend,' he said, deeply moved, but smiling, 'how it has all been put down correctly and according to the rules; only it can't be played because it's so extremely difficult that nobody would be able to play it.' 'That's why,' Wolfgang interrupted him, 'it's a concerto; you just have to practise it until you get it right. You see, it has to go like this.' He now began to play, but could only manage enough for them to gather what his ideas had been. For at that time he believed that to play a concerto and to work a miracle were one and the same thing; therefore his composition was a medley of notes that, although they were for the most part correctly put together, had been arranged in so difficult a fashion that even a master would have been unable to play them.

This story of the ink-blots has an additional interest, in that Mozart was pursued by them all his life. Throughout his correspondence he apologized time and again for his 'scrawls', bad handwriting, pens and paper. For Mozart was in all things a perfectionist and really longed to write a beautiful hand. This was impossible to him, chiefly owing to the speed with which his thoughts crowded on his fingers; he could never write down words or notes fast enough to get them on paper sufficiently quickly.

Leopold was certain that his son was an immortal genius and resolved later on to write Wolfgang's biography. To that end he carefully kept notes and diaries and when they went on their travels wrote long and detailed letters to his Salzburg friend and landlord, Lorenz Hagenauer, in which all the boy's early triumphs—fees, presents, and other emoluments—were recorded, and which Leopold charged Hagenauer to preserve for him. Fortunately this was done, although the proposed biography was never written.

2

The world into which Wolfgang Amadeus Mozart was born was a troubled one. His short life was lived during the second half of the eighteenth century, which included the Seven Years War, the loss of the American Colonies by England, and the great French Revolution. At his birth the Emperor Francis I and his consort, Queen Maria Theresa, were the absolutist rulers of Austria, Hungary and Bohemia. As an adult he lived during the reigns of the two following Hapsburg monarchs, Joseph II and Leopold II, mostly in Salzburg and later in Vienna, where he was commissioned to provide various works for state occasions.

Fortunately, although both as a child and a youth Mozart undertook several long concert tours, he himself was never exposed to the dangers of war. Leopold was a firm pacifist, strongly opposed to the rampant militancy of the day. He hated the brutal and insolent officer caste and despised the common and almost equally offensive soldiery. Wolfgang, whose character in early childhood and youth was moulded by his father, grew up with these antipathies and never lost them.

But in the eighteenth century peace as well as war had its dangers. This was the declining period of feudal rule, the pre-industrial age, when applied hygiene and medicine were still of a rough-and-ready kind. Mozart hated and feared most doctors almost as much as the military and not without reason.

Europe was then still in the main an agricultural continent, populated by an illiterate peasantry. The aristocracy and gentry were the main representatives of culture. Between them and the peasantry was only a thin wedge of educated citizens, who were to constitute the powerful middle-class, or *bourgeoisie*, of the following century, but who at that time still had very little social status. They were in the main lawyers, doctors, bankers, merchants, craftsmen, and artists. Professional musicians were included amongst the lowest ranks of all, only slightly above itinerant actors and other such 'beggars and vagabonds'. They depended for their livelihood on the bounty of royalty, princes of the church, or the great landed feudal aristocrats, such as the Hungarian Esterházys, whom Joseph Haydn served until middle-age, and to whom they were bound—if they were lucky enough to be engaged by them—under not very remunerative contracts. As members of the great households, when on duty they wore the liveries of their masters, and were considered no more highly from a social point of view than the cooks, valets and the rest of the lower and menial orders with whom they were placed at table.

In the capitals and other principal cities the architecture was often of surpassing beauty, but the hygienic conditions were menacingly primitive. In the huge and glorious Palace of Versailles—where the child Mozart played in 1763 to the King and Queen of France—there was a profusion of gold and crystal, but not one single 'modern convenience' for the thousands of courtiers and retainers who waited on the monarchs. The larger the building, the more glacial were the draughts that swept through it in winter time. The mansions even of the rich were dark, damp, and gloomy; only the reception rooms were illuminated at night by a myriad candles. Pitch-dark stairs and corridors were the rule. In England the window-tax had been introduced in 1696 and was increased six times between 1747 and 1808. Windows were seldom opened in winter in any case, as fresh air was regarded as highly dangerous, but in consequence of this tax many windows were bricked up, shutting out even more of the sunlight than previously.

These conditions, which were still worse in the picturesque but insanitary houses huddled together in the towns and villages, provided an ideal breeding-ground for tuberculosis. Open infected drains, beloved of rats, as well as contaminated water and milk, encouraged typhus and typhoid. Infants succumbed to disease and infection in their millions and their mothers, too, died in huge numbers in childbed, of puerperal fever, as they bore them into a world in which modern asepsis was as yet undreamed of. In the eighteenth century the expectation of life of a newly-born male infant was considerably less than thirty years.

The great and rich were no more immune from infection than the poor. In October 1767 the Austrian Archduchess Maria Josepha, about to be married to the King of Naples, died from smallpox. With his usual wry humour Leopold Mozart, then in Vienna with the children, wrote to Hagenauer: 'The Princess bride has become a bride of the Heavenly bridegroom. What an amazing change!'

The letters written by Mozart's father during the European tours on which he took his two little prodigies reveal his constant and very justifiable anxiety for their health. They did, in fact, catch measles, chicken-pox, the dreaded smallpox and even more dangerous scarlet fever, as well as various other fevers, internal upsets, sore throats and colds, all of which, however, they almost miraculously managed to survive.

A journey which is nowadays accomplished in a few hours by aeroplane—from Vienna to Paris, for instance—was in the eighteenth century a tremendous undertaking, with frequent daily stops and rests, by carriage or coach, drawn by two, four, or even six horses. News travelled commensurately slowly, most quickly by word of mouth, mixed up with rumour, or more reliably in the dispatches of diplomats or private bankers, sent by messengers. Letters went by 'post', not through a letter-box but by mail-coach, and sometimes took weeks to arrive, or frequently never arrived at all. The post was far too expensive to be utilized by any save the ruling classes and some members of the newly emerging middle class, to which the Mozart family belonged. In their correspondence there are constant allusions to and complaints of the high cost of it. Writing paper, also, was expensive and occasionally hard to come by; every scrap of it was precious and must not be wasted. In the circumstances it is indeed fortunate for posterity that neither Leopold nor Wolfgang allowed these difficulties to deter them from sending to one another, to their friends or relations, the most enormous letters, sometimes covering several large printed pages in their English translation and edition, filled not only with personal and professional information but with comments of all kinds—musical and theatrical criticisms, descriptions of people and places, financial and social accounts, and, in Wolfgang's case, delightful and occasionally even bawdy humour, jokes, and nonsense.

3

A glance at the map reveals that Salzburg was ideally situated geographically for the journeys Leopold Mozart was planning. He was not as yet looking southwards, towards Italy, but to the west and, at first, the small German states adjacent to Austria. His ambition for his little prodigies was to take them to France, and even to England. But Germany was the starting-point.

At that period Germany was split into several smaller or larger kingdoms, princedoms, and dukedoms, of which Prussia, in the north, was the most powerful, and Hanover to the north-west had given England a new dynasty. Unlike Austria and the South German states, the principal Northern states of Germany —Prussia and Hanover—had seceded from the Roman Catholic

Church and were firmly of the Lutheran or Protestant confession, which was also established in England. As a good and pious Catholic Leopold Mozart never felt completely at home in these heretical countries.

The first trial trip was made to the Court of the Elector Maximilian III of Bavaria, in Munich, and appears to have been a definite success.

There are no letters extant from Leopold describing his children's very first appearances in public. But we know that although certain of their royal admirers were musical, the prevailing taste was frivolous, in favour of light and amusing entertainment. The two 'cute' little Mozart children, the girl in her long stiff frock and the tiny boy in equally formal court finery, were regarded first and foremost as such musical tricksters and would probably have been just as much admired and petted by the flippant and sentimental ladies of the court had they been performing monkeys.

On this first occasion Leopold had not taken his children too far from home and their mother remained in Salzburg. But the second trip was planned by Leopold, who was a born impresario, to the Imperial Court in Vienna. They were to stay there for some time and so he decided to take his wife along to look after the family. They arrived in Vienna on 18 September 1762 and did not return to Salzburg until January 1763.

Wolfgang's fame as a prodigy had preceded him to Vienna from Salzburg and Munich, so that only a week after the family arrived in the capital they received a summons to appear at Court, before the Emperor Francis I and the Empress Maria Theresa and their family.

On 16 October Leopold wrote to his friend Hagenauer in Salzburg:

> Their Majesties received us with such extraordinary graciousness that when I shall tell of it people will declare that I have made it up. Suffice it to say that Wolferl jumped up on the Empress's lap, put his arms around her neck and kissed her heartily.

As a reward the children were each given a handsome costume:

Would you like to know what Wolferl's costume is like? It is of the finest cloth, lilac in colour. The waistcoat is of moiré, but of the same shade as the coat, and both coat and waistcoat are trimmed with wide double gold braiding. It was made for the Archduke Maximilian.

On his return to Salzburg Wolfgang was painted in this Court suit, by an Italian painter, Pietro Antonio Lorenzoni. This portrait cannot have been a very good likeness. The nose is too developed, the lips are too full, and the expression is not merely self-confident but positively critical. The impression that this is the picture of a gnome, a little elderly gentleman, is of course enhanced by the powdered hair and the clothes, which now seem like 'fancy dress' but which were in fact the regulation Court dress of the period. The royal fee for the concert—or 'present', for there was no fixed scale of remuneration in those days—was one hundred ducats, about £45. In his letters to Hagenauer, who was also acting as his banker, Leopold mentions two further fees of, respectively, twenty and six ducats, amounting altogether to about sixty pounds in English money, which would then, however, have been worth far more than at the present time. But against this, he pointed out, had to be set their daily minimum expenses of at least one ducat and the financial loss they shortly suffered, for Wolfgang caught scarlet fever on this first trip to Vienna. His father's anxiety for his health was increased by the financial disappointment this entailed, 'for in Vienna the nobility are afraid of pock-marks and all kinds of rash. So my boy's illness has meant a set-back of about four weeks'.

Wolfgang was, in fact, fortunate to have escaped from Vienna with his life. For only a month or two after their appearance at Court, 'Her Majesty the Empress has lost another Princess, the Princess Johanna, aged thirteen, who when we were at Court took my little Wolferl by the hand and led him through her rooms.' This little Princess died of typhus.

Such were the hazards of being an infant prodigy in 1762. But it is hardly surprising that a musician conditioned in early childhood to public performance and acclamation on such a scale should in later life have found it impossible to settle down in a small provincial cathedral city such as Mozart's native Salzburg.

4

The Mozart family returned home from Vienna in the new
year, but remained there only six months. The two trial runs
had been successfully accomplished and Leopold was now
ready to embark with his wife, Nannerl, and Wolfgang, on a
much more ambitious enterprise, a concert tour of Western
Europe which lasted two and a half years, from 9 June 1763
until 30 November 1766, from Wolfgang's seventh until his
tenth year. His father's application for this long leave of absence
was graciously granted by his employer, Archbishop von
Schrattenbach, and the family set out, taking the trip in easy
stages. This was not merely due to the necessity of feeding,
resting or changing the horses that drew their carriage, but
chiefly to enable the little prodigies to be seen and heard in the
various cities through which they passed.

They returned first to Munich. But these talented children
had already appeared there and Leopold's letters to Hagenauer
from Bavaria are full of grumbles, chiefly about the Elector's
dilatoriness in summoning his children to play again at Court
and then, in paying his 'present' or fee. And there were already
signs of rivalry, opposition and intrigue. For, wrote Leopold,
'I regard the whole business as the work of Jomelli'—(a Neapolitan composer and the local Court conductor)—'who is
doing his best to weed out the Germans at this Court and put
in Italians only.'

This opposition to Mozart on the part of the Italians was to
pursue him throughout his life. In his day, competition among
professional musicians was intense. This was due to the res-
tricted market—royal or smaller Courts or the homes of the
rich—open to them, and to the fact that the Italians had
already established a monopoly in it. And what they had they
fought, tenaciously and unscrupulously, to hold.

Leopold continued with complaints regarding the cost and
difficulties of transport, bad inns, and poor food. He was also
plagued, as modern travellers still are, by unfavourable rates of
exchange and by the many varieties of currency then prevalent,
such as ducats, thalers, groschen and kreutzer. But he took care
to furnish himself stage by stage with the necessary letters of
credit.

They arrived in Brussels in November. Here the same delays

occurred until they could obtain a hearing, 'for the Prince spends his time hunting, eating and drinking, and in the end it appears that he has no money'.

Nevertheless, this enforced idling was not wasted by Leopold. Avid sightseer that he was, he visited the great churches and cathedrals on his itinerary not only to worship there with his family, but to take Wolfgang to hear their Masses and glorious organs and, as well, to see and admire the great works of art that hung there, paintings by the famous Netherlands school and in particular by its greatest genius, Peter Paul Rubens.

And so, at last, to Paris, the Mecca of all eighteenth century culture. They arrived on 8 December and were invited to stay at the house of Count van Eyck, the Bavarian Minister to the King of France, whose wife was a daughter of Count Arco, Chief Chamberlain to the Archbishop of Salzburg.

Leopold, that Papa who was 'next to God' to little Wolfgang, disliked and mistrusted the French people and their whole way of life. Wolfgang must often have heard his father voice his views and feelings about them, as expressed by Leopold in a long and most interesting letter to Hagenauer's wife, written from Paris between 1 and 3 February, in which he recorded his provincial German's disapproval of social conditions in that great capital in pages that might with no disadvantage be placed next to those of a Victor Hugo or a Balzac a century later.

> And in addition to their idiotic '*mode*' in all things, there is their extreme love of comfort, which has caused this nation to turn a deaf ear to the voice of Nature. Hence everybody in Paris sends new-born children to be reared in the country. Persons both of high and low rank do this and pay a bagatelle for it. But you see the wretched consequences of this practice. For you will hardly find any other city with so many miserable and mutilated persons. You have only to spend a minute in a church or walk along a few streets to meet some blind or lame or limping or half-putrefied beggar, or to find someone lying on the street who had his hand eaten away as a child by the pigs, or someone else who in childhood fell into the fire and had half an arm burnt off while the foster-father and his family were working in the fields.

He further touched on the conflict between the Parliament and the priesthood, between the rival French and Italian schools of music, and the jealousy aroused in his own compatriots by Wolfgang's successes.

'The bulk of the country's wealth,' he wrote, 'is divided amongst about a hundred persons . . . and finally, most money is spent on Lucretias, who do not stab themselves . . . '

This allusion to Lucretia, the virtuous Roman matron who stabbed herself after having been raped by Tarquinius, is in fact, a veiled allusion to Madame de Pompadour, the King's famous mistress.

The Court was not in residence in Paris, but at the grandiose Palace of Versailles, which beggared even Leopold's powers of description. So the Mozart family had to present themselves there, where 'my children have taken almost everyone by storm'. Nevertheless when the matter of remuneration arose, 'everything goes at a snail's pace'.

The children had first performed to King Louis XV and the Queen, Maria Leszynska, who was Polish but spoke perfect German, and acted as interpreter between His Majesty and Wolfgang, the little prince charming of music. On New Year's Day Their Majesties dined in public and 'my Wolfgang was graciously privileged to stand beside the Queen the whole time, besides partaking of the dishes which she handed him from the table'.

Having been received by Their Majesties, Wolfgang and Nannerl were then taken to perform to Madame de Pompadour, who was in every respect the unofficial queen of France, and also a great patroness of artists and the arts. According to Leopold she was then 'still good-looking, tall and stately, or rather well-covered, but very well-proportioned, extremely dignified and uncommonly intelligent. Her apartments at Versailles are like a paradise'.

The children received valuable presents from various members of the aristocracy: 'Yesterday my boy got a gold snuff-box from Madam La Comtesse de Tessé' and 'from the Princesse Carignan a pocket writing-case in silver, with silver pens with which to write his compositions'. For in addition to all the successful performances they were giving Wolfgang was hard at work composing. He had written four sonatas for clavecin with violin accompaniment (K. 6-9) his first published works, of which Leopold wrote: 'At present four sonatas of M. Wolfgang

Mozart are being engraved. Picture to yourself the furore which they will make in the world when people read on the title-page that they have been composed by a seven-year-old child; and . . . imagine the sensation when he asks someone to write down a minuet or some tune or other and then immediately and without touching the clavier writes in the bass and, if it is wanted, the second violin part. In due course you will hear how fine these sonatas are; one of them has an Andante in a quite unusual style. Indeed I can tell you . . . that every day God performs fresh miracles through this child.'

Unfortunately, however, the miraculous child as well as his sister, caught a severe cold and sore throat. From these they recovered, but Leopold was indignant at the suggestion constantly being made to him that he should have Wolfgang inoculated against smallpox. Leopold did not agree with these new-fangled treatments: 'But for my part I leave the matter to the grace of God. It depends on His grace whether He wishes to keep this marvel of nature in the world in which he has placed it, or to take it to Himself. I shall certainly watch over it so well that it is all one whether we are in Salzburg or any other part of the world. But it is this watching that makes travelling expensive.'

The Mozart family, rigged out in their full Parisian finery, have been perpetuated in a portrait, a typical eighteenth-century 'conversation-piece', by the contemporary French painter, Louis de Carmontelle. In this water-colour, painted in 1763, Wolfgang, tiny as a dwarf, is at the harpsichord, his small legs dangling over the edge of the stool; Leopold stands behind him, playing the violin and Nannerl, holding a sheet of music, is behind the instrument.

The Paris visit came to a close at the end of April, when Leopold was ready to embark his family on their next great adventure, the crossing of the English Channel and the conquest of London.

Chapter II

LONDON

THE Mozart family arrived in England on 23 April 1764. Leopold had hired a boat to take them across the Channel. There were two servants as well as the family and in order to lighten the expense he agreed to take four other passengers as well. They were all sea-sick, 'but,' Leopold wrote to Hagenauer, 'we saved money, which would have been spent on emetics', (in those days one of the principal rough-and-ready remedies for internal upsets).

As usual, he complained of the heavy expenses as well as of the horde of porters who assailed the passengers as soon as they landed at Dover, and who tried to snatch their baggage from their own retainers, with loud cries of 'your most obedient servant, sir'.

The first impression which struck him on arrival in London was concerned with the strange clothes worn by the natives: 'In London everyone seems to me to be in fancy dress; and you cannot imagine what my wife and my little girl look like in English hats.' But there were other and deeper differences between the country they had just left and that in which they were to spend the next fifteen months.

The wars between Great Britain and France in the eighteenth century were not only concerned with the balance of power in Europe but chiefly, perhaps, with colonial expansionism and rivalry. It was an era of great naval as well as land battles. There were enormous prizes at stake, which included Canada on the North American continent and India in the Far East. The British had the best of these battles. Their American Colonies—which they were not to lose until much later in George III's reign—and the West and East Indies, in the latter of which the East India Company was opening up fabulous riches, were all contributing to the rising prosperity of the mother country and the emergence of an immensely wealthy aristocracy of trade and commerce.

So that it was to an increasingly prospering city that Leopold came in 1764 and in which the Mozarts—particularly Wolfgang—were remunerated with many golden guineas.

> On April 27th we were with the King and Queen . . . the present was only twenty-four guineas, which we received immediately on leaving the King's apartment . . . On May 19th we were again with the King and Queen . . . When we left the room we were again handed twenty-four guineas. If this happens every three or four weeks, we can put up with it!
>
> I have had another shock, that is, the shock of taking in one hundred guineas in three hours . . . The expenses are surprisingly great. But the profit will certainly not be less than ninety guineas . . . The hall without lighting or music stands costs five guineas. Each clavier, of which I had to have two, on account of the concerto for two claviers, costs half a guinea. The first violin gets three guineas and so on; and all who play the solos and concertos three, four and five guineas . . . But fortunately for me, all the musicians as well as the hall and everything else only cost me twenty guineas, because most of the performers would not accept anything.
>
> Once I leave England I shall never see guineas again. So we must make the most of our opportunity . . . But if I achieve the object which I have set myself, I shall haul in a fine fish or rather a good catch of guineas.

George III had succeeded his grandfather George II in 1760. The family were the hereditary Electors of Hanover, and when the first two Georges ascended the British throne they could speak little or no English. George III, however, was educated in England and spoke the language fluently, although with a somewhat thick German accent.

At the age of twenty-seven he had married a twenty-one-year-old German Princess, Charlotte of Mecklenburg-Strelitz.

There could hardly have been a greater contrast in royal styles of living than that between the courts of Louis XV in France, and George III in Great Britain. For the queen of Versailles, as we have seen, was not the Queen, but the royal mistress. The prevailing moral tone was, to say the least of it, flippant to the verge of cynicism. Luxury was carried to wild excess, extravagance publicly flaunted. And the country was running headlong into bankruptcy and revolution.

Across the Channel, however, no two more domesticated and

affectionate spouses could be found than the King and Queen; no scandal marred the stainlessness of their married life. George III is nowadays remembered with some contumely owing to his German pigheadedness and the loss of the American Colonies. But he more or less founded the great monarchical tradition of an impeccable family life, which Queen Victoria was to perpetuate in the next century and which has fortunately endured to our own day.

Queen Anne and the two former Georges had all been music patrons. From 1713 until 1759—five years before Wolfgang Mozart's arrival in London—the great George Frideric Handel had dominated the musical scene, providing the Court and society with a series of magnificent operas and oratorios for their delectation, of which *Messiah* was the crowning masterpiece. George III and his Queen had inherited his grandfather's passion for Handel's music.

Next in favour to Handel in the esteem of the Court and the public was Johann Christian Bach. He was the youngest son of Johann Sebastian Bach, the Leipzig organist who found favour with Frederick the Great of Prussia, but who at that time, when the 'galant' style of music was at the height of fashion, was known in England merely as the father of the great Johann Christian. After studying in Italy, the latter had settled in London and was music-master to the Queen. There were several other only slightly less popular German musicians then resident in the capital.

Opera, which meant Italian opera or opera in the Italian style, was almost a passion with the eighteenth-century London public. The eminent music historian Dr Charles Burney, friend of Dr Johnson and father of the novelist and diarist Fanny Burney, described the Italian operas then in vogue in no less than three hundred and forty pages. Not one of these operas still remains in the modern repertoire. Their importance in young Wolfgang Mozart's musical development, however, can hardly be overrated. Italian opera required, of course, Italian opera singers. In London Wolfgang for the first time in his life entered the world of Italian opera and opera singers. The most renowned among them was the male soprano, Manzuoli, who was enchanted with him and gave him singing lessons. And in no time at all Wolfgang was composing arias for him.

2

On arrival in London the Mozarts spent their first night at an inn in Piccadilly, the White Bear, and then found lodgings 'at the house of Mr Cousin, haircutter in Cecil Court, St Martin's Lane'.

As in Vienna and Paris they had not long to wait for a summons to Court:

> On April 27th we were with the King and Queen in the Queen's Palace in St James's Park; so that by the fifth day after our arrival we were already at Court . . . The graciousness with which both His Majesty the King and Her Majesty the Queen received us cannot be described. In short, their easy manner and friendly ways made us forget that they were the King and Queen of England. At all Courts up to the present we have been received with extraordinary courtesy. But the welcome which we have been given here exceeds all others. A week later we were walking in St James's Park. The King came along driving with the Queen and, although we all had on different clothes, they recognized us nevertheless and not only greeted us, but the King opened the window, leaned out and saluted us and especially our Master Wolfgang, nodding to us and waving his hand.

They went to Court again on 19 May,

> from six to ten in the evening. The King placed before him not only works of Wagenseil, but those of Bach, Abel and Handel, and he played off everything *prima vista*. He played so splendidly on the King's organ that they all value his organ-playing more highly than his clavier-playing. Then he accompanied the Queen in an aria which she sang . . . Finally he took the bass part of some airs of Handel (which happened to be lying there) and played the most beautiful melody on it and in such a manner that everybody was amazed.

It may have been the King and Queen who introduced the astounding child to Johann Christian Bach. They adored one another and one another's music. J. C. Bach had a considerable influence on Wolfgang's early compositions in consequence, and served him as a master in elegance and clarity of form.

After their right royal reception, the next step was infallibly a public concert, presumably the one at which Leopold had the pleasant 'shock' of raking in a hundred guineas.

An announcement of a later concert, which appeared in the
London *Daily Advertiser* on 9 April 1765, ran as follows:

> Mr Mozart, the Father of the celebrated young Musical
> Family, who have so justly raised the admiration of the greatest
> Musicians of Europe, intending soon to leave England, pro-
> poses, before his Departure, to give to the Public in general
> an Opportunity of hearing these young Prodigies perform
> both in public and private, by giving at the end of the month a
>   CONCERT
> Which will be chiefly conducted by his Son, a Boy of Eight
> Years of Age, with all the Overtures of his own Composition.
>
> Tickets may be had, at 5s. each, of Mr Mozart, at Mr
> Williamson's in Thrift Street, Soho; where such Ladies and
> Gentlemen, who chuse to come themselves, and take either
> Tickets, or the Sonatas composed by this Boy, and dedicated
> to Her Majesty (Price 10s. 6d.) will find the Family at home
> every Day in the Week, from Twelve to Two o'Clock, and
> have an Opportunity of putting his Talents to a more particular
> proof, by giving him any Thing to play at Sight, or any Music
> without a Bass, which he will write upon the Spot, without
> recurring to his Harpsichord.
>
> Notice of the Day, and Place of the Concert, will be given
> in due Time.

This advertisement seems to bear as much witness to
Leopold's talents as an impresario as to Wolfgang's musical
genius.

Dr Burney commented as follows: 'During his residence in
London we had frequent opportunities of witnessing his extraordinary talents and profound knowledge in every branch of
music at eight years old, when he was able to play at sight in
all clefs, to perform extempore, to modulate, and play fugues
on subjects given in a way that there were very few masters then
in London able to do.'[1]

The fact that the royal family preferred Wolfgang's organ-
playing even to his virtuosity on the harpsichord led to another
kind of concert, on 29 June 1764: 'There will be a concert or
benefit at Ranelagh in aid of a newly established Hôpital de

[1] Commenting on the advertisement, Dr Percy A. Scholes, in *The Great Dr
Burney*, wrote: 'As for the announcement that the concert would "chiefly be
conducted" by the boy, this means that it would be *carried through* by him. Baton-
conducting hardly existed then, and the boy would almost certainly sit at the
harpsichord, and so control the orchestra, though he may just possibly have
taken a violin and served as leader.'

femmes en couche, and whoever wishes to attend it must pay five shillings entrance. I am letting Wolfgang play a concerto on the organ at this concert in order to perform thereby the act of an English patriot who, as far as in him lies, endeavours to further the usefulness of this hospital which has been established *pro bono publico*. That is, you see, one way of winning the affection of this quite exceptional nation.'

During that summer the Mozarts were living in Chelsea, a salubrious village only two miles from London. They spent seven weeks there and lived in a house they had rented from a Dr Randal, in Fivefields Row. 'It has one of the most beautiful views in the world. Wherever I turn my eyes, I only see gardens and in the distance the finest castles; and the house in which I am living has a lovely garden.' The house in question is now 180 Ebury Street, London S.W.1. They had moved there because Leopold had caught what he described as the 'native complaint, which is called a "cold" '.

He had caught it on a very hot evening when the children were playing at Lord Thanet's. As it was a Sunday there were no hackney carriages for hire on their usual stand, so Leopold put the children into a sedan-chair and himself trotted behind it. Although on arrival he had hastened to put on his coat and button it up, with the usual lamentable English passion for fresh air all the windows had been left open and after having perspired 'as profusely as it is possible for a man to do', he caught this chill.

The seven weeks' stay in rural Chelsea seems to have done all the family good. During this time Wolfgang was by no means idle. He composed his first two symphonies, K.16 and 19, which were performed at the concert advertised by his father. They were in the Italian style then in fashion and certainly imitative of those similarly written by his friend and model, J. C. Bach. They nevertheless definitely foreshadowed Mozart's own later style.

In the following winter he wrote the six sonatas dedicated to Queen Charlotte. Leopold had them engraved and sold copies of them at the lodgings in Thrift Street (now Frith Street), Soho, where they lived on their return to town. He also sent copies of them to Hagenauer, to be advertised and put on sale in Salzburg.

3

Leopold was, as we know, a man of wide culture and interested in all the arts and many of the sciences. So he was particularly impressed, in London, with the British Museum, which had been founded twelve years previously. On a visit to that not then so venerable institution, Wolfgang presented to the Museum a setting of the words of the hymn 'God is Our Refuge'.

This is still in the Museum's Department of Printed Books. The official receipt for it ran as follows:

> Sir,
>
> I am ordered by the Standing Committee of the Trustees of the British Museum to signify to You that they have received the present of the Musical performances of your very ingenious Son, which You were pleased lately to make to them, and to return You their thanks for the same.
>
> M. MATY, Secretary, July 19th 1756.[1]

There was, however, an older and even more august institution then in existence in London, the Royal Society, which had been given its Royal Charter in 1662 by King Charles II. It published regularly volumes of *Philosophical Transactions* containing letters on matters of philosophical and later, increasingly, scientific interest, from correspondents in Great Britain and all over the world. Among these letters is one from the Honourable Daines Barrington, a son of the first Lord Barrington, who was a lawyer and later became a judge. He was also, however, an antiquary and naturalist and a keen amateur musician.

Not surprisingly, the extraordinary gifts of young Wolfgang Mozart had aroused the antagonism of many of his older professional rivals in the countries he visited. Leopold frequently complained of their disbelief that so young a child should be able to perform such astounding musical feats as his son did. In London as elsewhere, the story was put about that Leopold had lied about Wolfgang's age and that the boy was, in fact, a good deal older than he appeared to be.

Daines Barrington was fascinated by Wolfgang and his amazing genius and saw a good deal of him during his London

---

[1] Quoted from A. Hyatt King, *Mozart in Retrospect*, p. 90.

(a) Leopold Mozart. Painting probably by Pietro A. Lorenzoni, 1770

(b) Mozart's mother. Painting probably by Pietro A. Lorenzoni, 1775

[face p. 22

Salzburg, showing in the foreground the cathedral and part of the Archbishop's palace

visit. He waited, however, until four years afterwards, before he wrote his now famous letter to the Royal Society about him, which was published in the *Philosophical Transactions*.[1]

His reason for not sending it in sooner was, he explained, that with a lawyer's natural caution he preferred to wait until he could obtain irrefragable proof that Wolfgang had been only eight years and five months old at the time when Barrington had tested his musical knowledge and gifts. He finally obtained this proof in a birth certificate sent him by Leopold Comprecht, Chaplain to the Archbishop of Salzburg, dated 3 January 1769, and which he appended to his letter to the Secretary of the Royal Society, Matthew Maty—who was also, presumably Secretary to the Trustees of the British Museum.

In this certificate Wolfgang's birth date is given as 17 January 1756, and not 27, as we know it. His father, Leopold, is described as organist of His Highness, the Prince of Saltzbourg, and his mother's maiden name is given as Maria Ann Pertlin.

Barrington's letter is entitled 'Account of a very remarkable young Musician'.

His examination of Mozart consisted, first of all, in taking along to him a duet to words in Metastasio's libretto *Demofoonte*. The music which, says Barrington, it was absolutely impossible that he could have ever seen before, was composed by 'a gentleman'—presumably Barrington himself. The piece in question consisted of 'five parts'—accompaniments for first and second violin, two vocal parts, and a bass.

> The score was no sooner put upon his desk, than he began to play the symphony (overture) in a most masterly manner, as well as in the time and stile which corresponded with the intention of the composer . . . the greatest masters often fail in these particulars on the first trial.
>
> The symphony ended, he took the upper (vocal) part leaving the under one to his father. His voice in the tone of it was thin and infantine, but nothing could exceed the masterly manner in which he sung (*sic*). His father, who took the under part in this duet, was once or twice out, though the passages were not more difficult than in the upper one; on which occasions the son looked back with some anger, pointing out

[1] Vol. 60, 1770, p. 54, and which the present writer has been privileged to read.

to him his mistakes, and setting him right . . . he also threw
in the accompaniments of the two violins, wherever they were
most necessary, and produced the best effects . . .

When he had finished the duet, he expressed himself highly
in its approbation, asking with some eagerness whether I had
brought any more such music.

Having been informed, however, that he was often visited
with musical ideas, to which, even in the midst of the night,
he would give utterance on his harpsichord; I told his father
that I should be glad to hear some of his extemporary compositions.

The father shook his head at this, saying that it depended
entirely upon his being, as it were, musically inspired, but
that I might ask him whether he was in humour for such a
composition.

Happening to know that little Mozart was much taken
notice of by Manzoli, the famous singer . . I said to the boy
I should be glad to hear an extemporary *Love Song*, such as
his friend Manzoli might chuse in an opera.

The boy at this (who continued to sit at his harpsichord)
looked back with much archness, and immediately began
five or six lines of a jargon recitative proper to introduce a
love song.

He then played a symphony which might correspond with
an air composed to the single word *Affetto* . . .

I then desired him to compose a *Song of Rage*, such as might
be proper for the opera stage.

The boy again looked back with much archness, and began
five or six lines of a jargon recitative proper to precede a
Song of Anger . . . and in the middle of it he had worked himself
up to such a pitch that he beat his harpsichord like a person
possessed, rising sometimes in his chair.

. . . his execution was amazing, considering that his little
fingers could scarcely reach a fifth on the harpsichord.

Unfortunately there appears not to exist a single portrait of
Mozart, either as a child or later, that shows him smiling or
laughing. Yet this expression of 'much archness' was typical of
him. It twinkles through many of his letters. His wife Constanze
described him in later years to the Novellos, when they visited
her in Salzburg, as 'always so gay'. And the operas provide
sufficient evidence of his sense of humour. His comic characters,
Despina, Papageno, and especially the superb Osmin in *The*

Seraglio, embody it to perfection. Barrington's description reveals at what an early age Mozart's dramatic sense was already developed. The report continues:

> His astonishing readiness, however, did not arise merely from great practice; he had a thorough knowledge of the fundamental principles of composition, as, upon producing a treble, he immediately wrote a bass under it, which when tried, had a very good effect. He was also a great master of modulation, and his transitions from one key to another were excessively natural and judicious; he practiced in this manner for a considerable time with a handkerchief over the keys of the harpsichord.
>
> Witness as I was myself . . . I must own that I could not help suspecting that his father imposed with regard to the real age of the boy, though he had not only a most childish appearance, but likewise had all the actions of that stage of life.
>
> For example, whilst he was playing to me, a favourite cat came in, upon which he immediately left his harpsichord, nor could we bring him back for a considerable time.
>
> He would also sometimes run about the room with a stick between his legs by way of horse.
>
> . . . I am also informed that the Prince of Saltzbourg, not crediting that such masterly compositions were those of a child, shut him up for a week, during which he was not permitted to see anyone, and was left only with music paper and the words of an oratorio.
>
> During this short time he composed a very capital oratorio, which was most highly approved upon being performed.
>
> Mozart is now not much more than thirteen years of age.
>
> His extemporary compositions also, of which I was a witness, prove his genius and invention to have been most astonishing, least, however, I should insensibly become too strongly his panegyrist, permit me to subscribe myself
>
> Your most faithful
> Humble servant
> DAINES BARRINGTON

When making his report Barrington expressed the hope that little Mozart would not die young, as other prodigies had done, and that he would, like Handel, survive to a ripe age; for Handel, too, had been a prodigy, and composed church services at the age of nine.

Barrington's letter appeared, as he says, when Mozart was fourteen, and had long ago left England. That he need never have done so is revealed in a letter from Leopold to Hagenauer on 19 March 1765: 'I did not accept a proposal which was made to me. But what is the use of saying much about a matter upon which I have decided deliberately after mature consideration and several sleepless nights, and which is now done with, as I will not bring up my children in such a dangerous place (where the majority of inhabitants have no religion and where one only has evil examples before one). You would be amazed if you saw the way children are brought up here; not to mention other matters connected with religion.' In spite of this shocked outburst of Leopold's (the reason for which, apart from his religious prejudice, it would be interesting to know) Wolfgang retained the happiest memories of his visit to London.

Chapter III

VIENNA, 1767

THE homeward trip now began.

At the insistent request of the Dutch Ambassador to the Court of St James, Leopold agreed to make a short detour by way of Holland, in order that the children might be heard by the Prince of Orange and his sister, at The Hague. Nannerl was apparently the most enthusiastic supporter in the Mozart family of this plan. For when, in that autumn, she fell desperately ill, Leopold wrote grumpily to Hagenauer: 'I have seen her lying well-nigh *in extremis*. Yet who urged us to come to Holland more than my daughter? Indeed she had the greatest desire to go whither her fate was driving her.'

This resentment did not prevent him from suffering the most acute anxiety for her. Nannerl's illness, from which she happily recovered after a few weeks, seems to have been either pleurisy or pneumonia. Her parents nursed her devotedly and took care to give her both the best physical and spiritual ministers. At one moment her life was despaired of and she received extreme unction. She also received a well-intentioned homily from her mother and father, which is interesting as showing how used people were in the eighteenth and nineteenth centuries to losing their children on the threshold of youth, and how earnestly they took their duty of preparing them to leave this vale of sorrows for a better world; during 'the conversations which we three, my wife, myself and my daughter had on several evenings . . . we convinced her of the vanity of this world and the happy death of children . . . Meanwhile little Wolfgang in the next room was amusing himself with his music.'

Wolfgang was also ill in the following November, though less seriously so. His musical 'amusement' appears to have been, as usual, the work that was child's play to him. For in Holland he composed six sonatas for harpsichord with violin accompaniments (K. 26-31) for the Prince of Orange's sister, and two sets of variations for harpsichord (K. 24, 25). The children also, on their recoveries, played separately and together at Court. What one would have liked most to have heard, however, was Wolfgang's improvisation, for an hour, 'on the great organ in Haarlem, which is so famous'.

The children's illnesses as usual set Leopold back financially. Of Holland he wrote to Hagenauer: 'My present expenses are perfectly dreadful, for one must pay for everything. Everyone knows of course what Holland is. So heavy inroads are made on my purse', although he was impressed by the cleanliness 'which to many of us appears overdone' of Dutch towns and villages.

From Holland they returned to Paris in the spring of 1766, via Amsterdam and Utrecht (in both of which cities concerts were given), Rotterdam, Antwerp, Malines, Brussels, Valenciennes, and Cambrai, Leopold making suitable comments on local politics, art, and any other matter that happened to impress him. 'As we are now dressed again in black, one can see how my children have grown. We are all well. When we get back to Salzburg nobody, at first, will recognize little Wolfgang. It is a long time since we left and meanwhile he has seen and got to know many thousands of people.'

By the middle of August 1766 they were at Lyons, whence they travelled on to Geneva. In the following September they spent four days in Lausanne. In the previous chapter an account has been given of Daines Barrington's 'examination' of Mozart and his report on him to the Royal Society. Wolfgang must have by then—at the age of ten years and eight months— become used to being a subject of intense curiosity to the 'many thousands of people', to the scientists as well as music-lovers and scholars, he had been meeting during the past two years.

In Lausanne he was once again studied and described, by an anonymous admirer, and this description has also fortunately survived.[1]

The author prefaces his description of the boy by raising and attempting to answer the fascinating question of the origin of prodigies, whether musical or literary.

[1] The volume containing it is in the British Museum. The article in question has been translated and published in full by Mr A. Hyatt King, in his collection of erudite essays entitled *Mozart in Retrospect*.

It was not until 1874 that the Victorian anthropologist, Sir Francis Galton, attempted to distinguish between hereditary and environmental influences in human ability. But a century earlier Mozart's investigator was already trying to discriminate between and harmonize these influences in his case. 'Our little Orpheus', as he calls him

. . . was born with a marvellous ear and sensory organization disposed to be strongly affected by music: the son of a great musician and younger brother of a sister whose playing has shared your admiration; the first sounds he heard were harmonious ones; in him the sensitive string vibrated from childhood; at once it re-echoed sounds, and he must have composed music from the moment he heard any . . . He received at birth such keenness and delicacy of the organs that the slightest false note is painful to him . . . the sensitiveness and the precision of his ear are so great that discordant, shrill or too loud notes bring tears to his eyes. His imagination is as musical as his ear: it always hears many sounds together; one sound heard recalls instantaneously all those which can form a melodious sequence and a complete symphony . . . our young man . . . was sometimes involuntarily attracted to his harpsichord as by a secret force, and drew from it sounds which were the lively expression of the ideas with which he had just been occupied. One might say that at these moments he is himself the instrument in the hands of music and one may imagine him as composed of strings harmoniously put together with such skill that it is impossible to touch one without all the others being also set in motion . . .

This child is very natural; he is lovable, he has knowledge outside music, yet, if he were not a musician he would perhaps be only a very ordinary child. If he had not been born the son of a musician his talent might perhaps not have had the chance to develop till later on and his other faculties would have remained buried until that time.

We can confidently predict that one day he will be one of the greatest masters of his art; but is it not to be feared that, developing so young, he may grow old prematurely?[1]

. . . I should fail in what I owe to your views if I did not remind you for one moment of the moral qualities of the child, which have much more claim to your interest. His heart is as sensitive as his ear; he has a modesty rare at his age, rare with that superiority. We are indeed edified on hearing him ascribe his talents to the author of every gift, and conclude, with amiable candour and the most

---

[1] A tragic and amazingly accurate prediction.

persuasive air, that it would be unpardonable for him to boast of them. We cannot see without emotion all the marks of his affection for a father who seems worthy of it, who has given still more care to the formation of his character than to the cultivation of his talents . . . how delightful it is for him to see his two amiable children more flattered by a look of approbation in his eyes which they seek with tender anxiety than by the applause of a whole audience . . . it would be very desirable that parents whose children have outstanding talents should imitate M. Mozart, who, far from forcing his son, has always been careful to moderate his ardour and so prevent him from abandoning himself to it.[1]

2

The Mozart family finally arrived home in Salzburg from their brilliantly successful tour on 30 November 1766. Their reluctance to return is foreshadowed in a letter from Leopold to Hagenauer from Lyons in the previous August, and in another one from Munich, on 15 November: 'Don't you think it very heroic and magnanimous of us to have decided to abandon a trip to Turin, which lies almost in front of us? Don't you think that its proximity, our circumstances, the general encouragement to do so and our own interest and love of travel ought to have induced us to follow our noses and go to Italy . . . now is the time when my children on account of their youth can arouse the admiration of everyone. However . . . I have promised to go home and I shall keep my word.

' . . . who knows what plans are being made for us after our return to Salzburg? Perhaps we shall be received in such a way that we shall be only too glad to shoulder our bundles and clear out.'

During his absence of two and a half years Leopold had continued to be a servant of the Archbishop, and drew a salary for services he was not in a position to perform. Von Schrattenbach was, however, kind and easy-going and made no objections, even when less than a year after their homecoming the Mozart family again left Salzburg, this time for Vienna, where they remained for another year and four months.

The Emperor Francis I had died in 1765, during their residence in London. His widow, Maria Theresa, ranks with

[1] Op. cit., pp. 316-7.

Elizabeth I of England and with Maria Theresa's contemporary, Catherine the Great of Russia, as one of the outstanding female rulers in history. She was the eldest daughter of the Emperor Charles VI, an Archduchess of Austria, and succeeded as Queen of Hungary and Bohemia. She had sixteen children—five sons and eleven daughters. But a woman could not be crowned Emperor of the Holy Roman Empire by the Pope, and when the Emperor Francis died he was succeeded as such by their eldest son, Joseph II. Mother and son now ruled jointly over their vast empire. It was an uneasy partnership; in view of the divergencies between their ages, sexes, characters and temperaments it could hardly have been otherwise.

Maria Theresa resembled Queen Victoria of England in her firm, almost priggish standards of morality. She permitted not the slightest moral laxness in women and set up an elaborate spy system to report to her the least delinquencies of any lady of her Court and even of the city of Vienna, mercilessly persecuting any unfortunate female who incurred her displeasure. Although she considered herself a perfect mother, she was ruthless, even towards her own daughters. They became mere pawns in her political plans. They were married off in their early 'teens to kings or princes with whom Maria Theresa thought it expedient to ally herself. The most famous of these marriages ended most tragically, when pretty, silly little Marie-Antoinette, whom her mother had paired off with King Louis XVI of France solely in the interest of the Franco-Austrian alliance, died on the guillotine.

The ostensible reason for the Mozart family's visit to Vienna in 1767 was the betrothal of another of Maria Theresa's daughters, the Archduchess Maria Josepha, to the King of Naples. Leopold hoped that his children would be engaged to perform during the festivities connected with the marriage. Like Andrew Marvell 'To His Coy Mistress' Leopold might have said that 'at my back I always hear Time's wingèd chariot hurrying near', and he did in fact say so less poetically when he wrote to Hagenauer that 'Every moment I lose is lost forever. And if I ever guessed how precious for youth is time, I realize it now.' He was not merely mercenary, as has been said; his belief in Wolfgang's genius was steadfast. But in his realistic way he foresaw correctly that the older the boy grew the less interest he would arouse in the wealthy but non-musical public, with the consequent decline in emoluments and 'presents'. It was for this reason that Leopold was already laying his plans for Wolfgang's thorough musical education, which was to involve several prolonged visits to Italy. But if these ambitions were to fructify, something more than an assistant-conductor's salary would be required to pay for his son's studies, and he hoped that once again Wolfgang would receive a large number of profitable engagements.

But the second Viennese visit was not to repeat the success of the first. It started off badly with the death of the young Archduchess from smallpox, which at that time was raging in the city. The Mozarts were lodging with a goldsmith, three of whose children had caught the disease. Leopold, panic-stricken, tried frantically to get Wolfgang away in time, but in vain. They fled to Brünn, and then on to Olmütz, but in the Black Eagle Inn there the child became desperately ill. However, a Count Podstatsky earned Leopold's profound gratitude by taking the whole family, including the sick boy, into his home.

Both Nannerl and Wolfgang in due course made good recoveries from the disease and by the beginning of January 1768, the family were once more in Vienna. Leopold had now formed a new scheme. He was attempting to get his young son commissioned to write an opera to be produced in the capital.

Once the smallpox epidemic had run its course Wolfgang was again most kindly received at Court, and, as Leopold wrote to Hagenauer, it was the Emperor himself who first suggested the plan. It may have been more or less in jest that Joseph II asked little Mozart if he would like to compose an opera and conduct it himself. Wolfgang—and his father—took the suggestion quite seriously. For he had already composed operatic airs for Manzuoli in London and, as Barrington's examination proved, had considerable command even then over this most difficult of all musical media. But the impresario in charge of the Viennese Court entertainments, again an Italian, Giuseppe Affligio, was no more enthusiastic about the project than Mozart's rival composers.

A librettist, Marco Coltellini, was found and the opera was to be called *La Finta Semplice*. But there now ensued a long and violent struggle on Leopold's part to have the work put on. He poured out his woes and rage with Affligio, who sabotaged him successfully at every turn, in an enormous and furious letter to Hagenauer. But the producer cannot be judged too harshly for being reluctant to stage a work, written by a boy of twelve, when so many adult composers (most of them his own hungry compatriots) were competing for his stage.

Matters were not made easier by the fact that Archbishop Schrattenbach was getting tired of having on his pay-roll an assistant-conductor who for years at a time had been drawing a salary which he had done nothing to earn. Leopold was informed by the Chief Steward that he would be paid up to March 1768, 'but that in future when he is not actually in Salzburg he will be retained as before in the Archbishop's service, but during his absence will not be paid his usual salary'. The struggle to get *La Finta Semplice* produced dragged on until the beginning of 1769, when Leopold was obliged to submit to defeat and even to petition the Archbishop to have his arrears of salary restored.

Wolfgang, however, had by no means been wasting his time in Vienna. As usual he had been busily composing, among other works a little operetta called *Bastien and Bastienne*. This was performed in the private theatre of a wealthy and fashionable Doctor Mesmer, who was a good friend and patron to the Mozarts and who is himself remembered in medical history as the discoverer of so-called 'mesmerism', an early form of psychological treatment.

The Archbishop proved himself well-disposed towards the little Salzburg prodigy, for on the family's return he ordered a special performance in his palace of *La Finta Semplice*. Wolfgang was rewarded with the title of Konzertmeister, though he was paid no salary. During the rest of that year he remained at home, studying and perfecting himself both in composition and execution, and wrote a couple of Masses and a Cassation, or suite.

Leopold obstinately nursed his next plan, meanwhile. This was to take Wolfgang to Italy, both as performer and student. The requisite leave was again granted and they set out— leaving Mama Mozart and Nannerl at home this time— on 12 December 1769.

Chapter IV

ITALY

ITALY, like Germany, was not then an independent sovereign state. By the treaty of Aix-la-Chapelle large portions of Italian territory had been parcelled out between Spain, France, and Austria, which had taken the lion's share, including the whole of Lombardy.

The Mozarts set out in high spirits for this lovely country, with a glorious climate, in which the arts flourished as gaily as the fruits and flowers of the earth. Wolfgang was now old enough to write his own letters, and Leopold's Italian correspondence is supplemented by notes and postscripts from him to his mother and sister, hastily written when he could snatch sufficient time from his strenuous activities as composer, performer, and musical scholar. They reveal his delight in the journey, his perennial good humour and merriment, his high spirits and intelligence. They show that he already had a fluent command of French and Italian, as well as his native German, for as his Swiss admirer had pointed out, Leopold had given him a good general as well as musical education.

His letters home were mostly concerned with operas he saw, their leading performers, and the arias they contained. But Leopold, that keen sightseer, managed to find time for them both to visit all the principal museums, galleries, and, of course, churches. From Rome Wolfgang wrote, with the self-mockery and gaiety that were so typical of him even as a growing boy:

> I have had the honour of kissing St Peter's foot in St Peter's church and as I have the misfortune to be so small, I that same old dunce,
>
> Wolfgang Mozart
> had to be lifted up.

Leopold assiduously kept a travel diary and Wolfgang also occasionally noted down his own impressions. At the outset of the trip he wrote delightedly to his mother: 'My heart is completely enchanted with all these pleasures, because it is so jolly on this journey, because it is so warm in the carriage and because our coachman is a fine fellow who, when the road gives him the slightest chance, drives so fast.' Travel stimulated him creatively all his life and now, in the inn at Lodi, he composed his first string quartet, K. 7.

They went by way of Rovereto, Mantua, and Cremona (famous for its violins) to Milan, stopping, as usual, in every one of these cities to be seen and heard. His organ-playing and composing aroused the warm-hearted Italians to such enthusiasm that poems were composed in his honour. In Verona his portrait was painted by Cignaroli. This is the first one that appears to be a good likeness, and shows Wolfgang, at fourteen, as charming as the young page, Cherubino, in *The Marriage of Figaro*. He is wearing one of his fine suits (such as the one described by Leopold) of 'apple-green shot moiré, with silver buttons and lined with rose-coloured taffeta, and his diamond ring'. Leopold wrote to his mother: 'Everything he wears is rather tight for him and he has removed all the silk threads which were wound round his diamond ring . . . But you must not think that he has grown very tall. It is only that his limbs are becoming bigger and stronger. He has no longer any singing voice. It has gone completely . . . He is most annoyed, for he can no longer sing his own compositions, which he would sometimes like to do.'

In the portrait Wolfgang is seated at the harpsichord, on which is one of his own compositions, looking towards his audience with a blend of modesty and self-confidence, an expression typical of him throughout his life.

When they arrived in Milan the Mozarts hastened to pay their respects to Count Firmian, the Governor-General of Lombardy and a native of Salzburg. They remained in that city as his guests and the Count gave a brilliant party for Wolfgang. Much more important, however, both to him and to Leopold was that as the result of this soirée, for which he had composed four arias to words by Metastasio, the foremost librettist of the day, he was engaged to write an opera for the following season.

After this great success they went on to Bologna, which was one of their principal points of pilgrimage in Italy. For here lived the most famous eighteenth-century teacher of music, the great scholar Padre Martini. He was already elderly and had heard a great many ambitious young musicians. To be approved of by him was to receive the highest hallmark of distinction both as composer and performer. Padre Martini received young Mozart very kindly. But when he found that the boy passed every test he set him with the greatest ease and brilliance his kindness was reinforced by astonishment and admiration. He further showed his interest in Wolfgang when he came to a concert given in Mozart's honour by the local grandee, Count Pallavicini: 'Padre Martini, the idol of the Italians,' wrote Leopold, 'speaks of him with great admiration and has increased his reputation all over Italy.'

And so on to Florence, where they met one or two old friends. The Archduke Leopold, younger brother and heir to the Emperor, Joseph II, remembered hearing little Mozart at Court in Vienna and now received him very kindly. Their other old friend, whom, to their mutual delight they accidentally met in the street, was the male soprano Manzuoli, for whom Wolfgang had written his first vocal works in London.

In Florence Wolfgang also made a new friend and—rare event for our young touring virtuoso—one of his own age. In Salzburg he did have one or two friends amongst his contemporaries, but he had spent very little of his childhood there. The boy he now met was English; his name was Thomas Linley, son of Mr Linley of Bath and brother of the lovely Miss Elizabeth Linley who eloped with and married the wit and playwright Richard Brinsley Sheridan. Thomas Linley too was a prodigy, an exquisite violinist who had gone to Florence to study there with Nardini, who had a world reputation as the greatest fiddler of the day. Leopold Mozart was also an authority on the instrument and his text-book or *Violinschule* was very highly regarded. Although Wolfgang had by that time almost given up the violin in order to concentrate on keyboard instruments and on composition, he was still an excellent performer on it. He and Thomas Linley were exactly the same age —fourteen—and according to Leopold even the same size. The two boys spent a whole evening as well as the following afternoon playing violin duets together, 'not like boys', wrote Leopold, 'but like men. Little Tommaso accompanied us home and wept bitter tears because we were leaving on the following day.'

Another English visitor to Florence at that time was Dr Burney. In his book entitled *The Present State of Music in France and Italy* he wrote of Wolfgang and Master Linley: 'The *Tommasino*, as he is called, and the little Mozart, are talked of all over Italy as the most promising geniuses of this age.'

Their paths in life diverged and they never met again. Thomas returned to Bath and a successful musical career in England, which came to a tragic and premature end, for at the age of twenty-two he was accidentally drowned. Mozart was later on to have other English friends whom he also loved and to whom he often spoke with sorrowful affection of this charming and delightful musician.

The Mozarts proceeded, in wicked weather and under very trying conditions, from Florence to Rome. Leopold's letter to his wife from the Holy City on 14 April 1770, contains an account of an amusing incident: 'On the 12th we were present at the Functiones, and when the Pope was serving the poor at table we were quite close to him . . . This incident was all the more amazing as we had to pass through two doors guarded by Swiss guards in armour and make our way through many hundreds of people. And moreover you must note that we had as yet no acquaintances. But our fine clothes, the German tongue, and my usual freedom of manner which led me to make my servant order the Swiss guards in German to make way for us, soon helped us through everywhere. They took Wolfgang for some German courtier, while some even thought that he was a prince, which my servant allowed them to believe; I myself was taken for his tutor.'

And they attended the famous performance in the Sistine Chapel of the *Miserere* by the seventeenth-century composer Gregorio Allegri. Very few copies of this work existed. But Wolfgang memorized it completely at a first hearing and on his return home wrote it down from beginning to end. He also found time to write to Nannerl: 'Please try to find the arithmetical tables. You know that you wrote them down yourself. I have lost my copy and so have quite forgotten them. So I beg you to copy them out for me with some other examples in arithmetic and send them to me here.'

The Romans soon heard with amazement of his feat in writing down the *Miserere* and it led to several concert engagements, for which he composed three symphonies as well as two soprano airs.

From Rome they went on to Naples, where their successes in royal and aristocratic circles were again repeated. Leopold described to his wife their 'beautifully braided summer costumes. Wolfgang's is of rose-coloured moiré . . . it is trimmed with silver lace and lined with sky-blue silk'. They were received by 'the English Ambassador, Hamilton, a London acquaintance of ours, whose wife plays the harpsichord with unusual feeling . . . She trembled at having to play before Wolfgang'. This was Sir William Hamilton, but the lady in question was his first wife and not the beautiful and notorious Emma who became the mistress of Lord Nelson.

Professional success, the southern sun, an excursion on the Mediterranean and other amusements all kept Wolfgang in great spirits. He wrote several letters to Nannerl, switching gaily from Italian to French and then 'Let us talk Salzburgish for a change, for it is more sensible'. To his mother he wrote: 'I too am still alive and always merry as usual and I simply love travelling.'

Leopold boasted to his wife in a letter from Rome, how on the return journey from Naples he 'announced everywhere that I was the steward of the Imperial Ambassador . . . Thus not only did I ensure a safe journey, but I was given good horses and quick service; and at Rome it was not necessary for me to go to the Customs Office for the usual examination, for at the gate I was received with a deep bow, and was simply told to drive on to my destination . . . As we had only slept for two out of the twenty-seven hours of our journey and had only eaten four cold roast chickens and a piece of bread in the carriage, you can well imagine how hungry, thirsty and sleepy we were . . . Wolfgang sat down on a chair and at once began to snore and to sleep so soundly that I completely undressed him and put him to bed without his showing the least sign of waking up . . . When he awoke at nine o'clock in the morning he did not know where he was nor how he had got to bed.'

In Rome Wolfgang was granted the honour of a special audience with the Pope, who invested him with the Order of the Golden Spur, which carried with it the title of 'Cavaliere', 'the same as Gluck has', Leopold wrote with pardonable pride.

Mozart at the age of fourteen. Oil painting by Saverio dalla
Rosa, 1770

[face p. 38

Mozart wearing the Order of the Golden Spur (1777); artist
unknown

But Wolfgang never used his title. For he was a professional musician to his finger-tips and musical success mattered far more to him than social distinction.

Another such success awaited him in Bologna, which was then famed throughout the world for its university and musical academy. And now Wolfgang presented himself there for a severe examination. The candidates had to be over twenty-one years of age, but an exception was made in Wolfgang's case and justifiably, for he passed all the difficult tests set him in less than an hour and was acclaimed by his examiners. Padre Martini also gave him a formal testimonial after he had solved a further series of problems in advanced counterpoint.

It was now time, however, for him to begin to work seriously on his opera that was to be produced in Milan. The first problem was to find a libretto or book, that would fit the available singers, chiefly the leading soprano and the principal man. Wolfgang, as he did all his life, aimed high. He hoped for a libretto from Metastasio and that Manzuoli would take one of the chief roles. But he had to content himself with lesser lights. The libretto finally chosen was called *Mitridate, Rè di Ponto*, by Cigna-Santi.

As Italian operas of the period were generally 'tailored' to suit the available singers, Mozart did not write the leading man's arias until after his arrival in Milan in October. Throughout his life he was to write parts of his operatic works—the greatest as well as the least of them—at fever heat, sometimes at the very last moment, even during rehearsal. For this early work he was to be paid one hundred cigliati—about £45— and free lodging as his fee.

The Italian operatic public and especially the Milanese was, according to our modern conventions, a very strange one indeed. The audiences came, not to witness drama, but to enjoy vocal fireworks, as certain opera enthusiasts do even to our own day, or not to listen at all, but to indulge in social activities. Italian opera of the eighteenth century can be roughly divided into two sections, the serious, or *opera seria*, based on a classical or solemn theme, and the comic or *opera buffa*. In his later operatic works Mozart was to reveal the full heights of his genius by deepening and broadening both these forms, and above all to create individual, intensely human characters, both tragic and gay, whose personalities were presented through and became inseparable from the music with which they were identified. But now, and throughout his early years as an operatic composer, he had to make do with the stock figures expected by public convention, such as the 'heavy', noble or absurd father, the innocent and preferably persecuted heroine, the chivalrous hero, and in addition, to fit their music to the demands made on the composer by its interpreters for plenty of opportunity for vocal display.

During the closing months of 1770 both Wolfgang and Leopold were feeling the strain. Owing to Count Firmian's protection they did not suffer the same degree of sabotage as in Vienna, but there were nevertheless worries in plenty. At the end of October the leading man had still not been engaged. The prima donna had been told that a boy of fourteen could not possibly provide her with suitable arias and had been given others, to insert into her part. But when Wolfgang played his over to her, she accepted them without demur. There was quite a large orchestra, which Mozart conducted for the first three performances, seated at the first harpsichord, as was the usage. He had a new suit made for this occasion, of scarlet trimmed with gold braid and lined with sky-blue satin.

The first performance of *Mitridate* was given on 26 December, and fortunately it was a success, so much so that Wolfgang received two further commissions; to write a dramatic serenata for the wedding of Maria Theresa's son, the Archduke Ferdinand, who was to be married in Milan in October of the following year, and an opera for the Milanese carnival season early in 1773.

There now followed a brief holiday, a visit to Venice on the way home. 'We shall soon have had enough of gondolas. During the first days the whole bed rocked in our sleep,' the unromantic Leopold informed his wife. But Wolfgang thoroughly enjoyed himself with his hostess and her six daughters, who tried to make him 'submit to the *attaco*, that is, having his bottom spanked when he is lying on the ground, so that he may become a true Venetian. They tried to do it to me—the seven women all together—and yet they could not pull me down.' Whether or not it was this harmless horseplay that shocked him, Leopold regarded Venice as 'the most dangerous place in all Italy', and indeed it was as famed for the looseness of its women's morals as for its scenic beauties.

They arrived home at the end of March and Wolfgang was soon hard at work as ever composing, chiefly church music and symphonies. By the beginning of August it was time to return to Milan for the serenata. He was now fifteen and once again showed his incredible facility and speed in composition. For the libretto did not arrive until the end of the month. On 13 September Leopold wrote to his wife that 'In twelve days, Wolfgang, with God's help, will have completely finished the serenata', but it is hardly surprising that on the 21st he himself wrote to Nannerl that his fingers ached from so much composing. Moreover, 'upstairs we have a violinist, downstairs another one, in the next room a singing-master who gives lessons, and in the other room opposite ours an oboist. That is good fun when you are composing! It gives you plenty of ideas.'

Ascanio in Alba was not an opera in the strict sense, but an operatic entertainment, with solo singing, choruses, and a great deal of ballet. On this occasion he was able to get Manzuoli to sing the principal part. The work was produced on 13 October and repeated several times with great success. In addition to his fee, the composer was presented by his royal patrons with a watch set in diamonds.

At the end of December they were once again in Salzburg. Early in the New Year Wolfgang fell ill, partly no doubt due to physical fatigue and lack of resistance brought on by overwork. Leopold had frequently alluded in his letters to his wife to their son's untidiness or forgetfulness—'you know what he is'— and this was a recurring complaint in later years as well. Indeed, throughout Mozart's youth and manhood it never seems to have occurred to anyone, that, slave as he was to his creative gift and to the exhausting physical work it entailed, he should have been shown some leniency with regard to the trivial matters he occasionally forgot or neglected. He was now no longer a child prodigy but at the period of adolescence, which today is recognized to be one that may involve great emotional and sometimes physical stresses, yet he was expected to conform to adult standards of composition and performance. That he was able to do so with the greatest brilliance did not lessen the weariness brought on by constant writing, covering sheet after sheet with notes for hours at a time. Leopold watched over him with great care and was of invaluable help to him as courier, secretary, and impresario. But that did not prevent him from behaving towards his son in other matters like any middle-class father of the period, with merciless strictness.

In the spring of 1772 an event occurred which was to have a profound effect on the whole of Mozart's subsequent life. Archbishop von Schrattenbach, who had so constantly granted Leopold and Wolfgang leave of absence, died. He was succeeded on 14 March by Hieronymus Count von Colloredo, member of a great and powerful family, who was to be a far less complaisant employer of the Mozarts. For the time being, however, their routine remained as before. Throughout the spring and summer Wolfgang continued to compose—until, in October, father and son set out once again for Milan, where the new opera for the carnival, *Lucio Silla*, was written and produced at the end of December, once again with great success.

The strain of all these years of travel was beginning to tell on Leopold. During their second Italian trip he had injured a leg which had taken some time to heal. He was now fifty-four and in his letters to his wife he constantly complained of his rheumatism, his misery and discomfort, and the impossibility of returning home over the icy, snow-bound roads of the Tyrol. Some of his complaints were genuine enough, but those letters were not, in fact, as ingenuous as they were meant to appear.

PART TWO: YOUTH

Chapter V

WILD OATS

IN his letter to his wife from Milan, dated 30 January, 1773, Leopold, after bitter complaints about the weather and his ailments, added a postscript in the family cipher which they used when they wrote confidentially to one another, as they feared that their correspondence might be opened and read by the archiepiscopalian spies. (Wolfgang also occasionally used this simple cipher in his later letters to his father.) The postscript ran: 'What I wrote about my illness is all quite untrue. I was in bed for a few days, but now I am well and off to the opera this evening. You must, however, spread the news everywhere that I am ill. You should cut off this scrap of paper so that it may not fall into the hands of others.' For some reason Frau Mozart omitted this precaution.

There was a good reason for Leopold's little intrigue in this matter. He himself was a highly competent musician. Yet since he had entered the service of Archbishop von Schrattenbach he had never advanced very far. Miraculously, a musical phoenix had arisen from the ashes of his own ambitions, and Wolfgang's career had become his father's chief preoccupation. Now—in 1773—he was seventeen and Leopold had been taking thought for some time about finding his son a lucrative appointment elsewhere than in Salzburg. It was, however, essential that no hint of his intentions became known to his employers, and illness was his excuse for his procrastination in returning home. Wolfgang's brilliant successes in Italy had led him to hope that they might lead to some permanent engagement; but, alas, they never did. Presumably even under the Hapsburg domination the Italians would not have tolerated such foreign competition. Nor was Mozart ever again invited to perform or create another opera there. They were therefore obliged to return to Salzburg in the spring of 1773, where the new Archbishop, Colloredo, had been installed the year previously.

It is almost impossible for anyone living in the democratic

modern world to appreciate fully the pomp and circumstance of the royal courts of the eighteenth century, with their iron protocol and strict adherence to social precedence and convention. They also set the tone for the great landowners and the princes of the church. The reaction against this world of privilege had even then already begun, ushered in by the French intellectuals; by the works of Voltaire, Rousseau, and Caron de Beaumarchais, author of the great satirical play *Le Mariage de Figaro*.

Hieronymus Colloredo, son of a former Vice-Chancellor to the Imperial Court, immensely rich and powerful, affected to be an admirer of those revolutionary thinkers Rousseau and Voltaire, whose portraits hung on the walls of his study. He was undoubtedly intelligent and insufferably arrogant as well. When he succeeded the good-natured old von Schrattenbach the inhabitants of Salzburg were far from pleased. And in his dealings with his underlings, including his court musicians, he tolerated neither disrespect nor insubordination. In Rome, only a year or so previously, Wolfgang had been mistaken for a young prince, and had been received and decorated by the Holy Father. But to Colloredo the Mozarts—father and son— were simply two bumptious little men with ideas above their station. They were thus confronted with all the might and power of this implacable social superior, whom they could only address in the most humble terms—in the third person plural— and approach via his court officials.

Wolfgang's violent discontent with this situation was not only the result of his consciousness of his own genius and his successes as a prodigy, but also reflected Leopold's permanent sense of frustration. There is little doubt that even had Wolfgang not been so much more gifted than his father, this bitterness would still have been absorbed by him throughout his childhood and youth, together with everything else Leopold had inculcated into him, such as religious and filial piety and the highest professional integrity. The only difference between them, in their long-drawn-out struggle with Colloredo, was Wolfgang's youthful optimism as opposed to Leopold's middle-aged pessimism, and his proud consciousness of his unique talent, notwithstanding the great world's reluctance to accept him at his own valuation.

The year 1773 marked a kind of watershed in Mozart's creative life. When he returned from his last trip to Italy his compositions in Salzburg—five symphonies, a divertimento for wind instruments, a concerto for two violins and another mass—were still written under Italian influence. But in July Colloredo left Salzburg for a visit to Vienna, and his two musicians did the same, taking as it were 'French leave' during his absence. It was then that Wolfgang for the first time came under the influence of the musical style of his great contemporary and elder Joseph Haydn. He was the brother of Leopold's colleague, Michael Haydn, organist to the Archbishop of Salzburg. Joseph had for many years been chief conductor and composer to the great Hungarian landowners, the Princes Esterházy. Unlike so many of their contemporaries, the Esterházys were generous and genuine music-lovers. Joseph Haydn, one of the most charming of men and composers, lived very happily at Eisenstadt and on the Esterházy estates for more than thirty years, with an occasional visit to Vienna during the winter. And there he wrote in a musical idiom native to him, which became the basis of the new German style.

It was during this summer in Vienna that Mozart heard a series of Haydn's quartets which had a profound influence on his own style from that time onwards. He had not, of course, gone to Vienna for this purpose, but once again in the hope of obtaining some appointment, a hope that was once again ungratified. In October Leopold and Wolfgang were back in Salzburg, where he continued to compose and to develop his own musical idiom with increasing brilliance.

As a child Wolfgang had been proficient both on the violin and on the keyboard instruments. When he grew older, although he wrote several exquisite violin concertos, his father's instrument became less congenial to him. The forte piano, as the early pianos were called, became, after the organ, his favourite instrument. He wrote twenty-five piano concertos in all, the first of them in this year.

Yet opera remained his greatest passion. He began to compose some incidental music to a contemporary play, *Thamos, King of Egypt*, but did not finish it. For he had been asked to write a new opera for the Munich carnival of 1775, and this

work, *La Finta Giardiniera*, was produced there in January
of that year. It was a great success, but the Archbishop only
arrived in Munich after the production, and was quite clearly
uninterested in it. Leopold wrote with some bitterness to his
wife: 'Picture to yourself the embarrassment of the Archbishop
at hearing the opera praised by the whole family of the Elector
and by all the nobles, and at receiving the enthusiastic con-
gratulations which they all expressed to him. Why, he was so
embarrassed that he could only reply with a bow of the head
and a shrug of the shoulders.' But this was mere wishful
thinking on Leopold's part, for the shrug was probably one of
indifference to the talents of the young musician whose services
he commanded, and who, after this success, once more resumed
his duties in Salzburg. Rumours had by now begun to spread
there that Wolfgang Mozart was trying to find another post;
Leopold wrote to his wife to deny them.

But what was Wolfgang's future to be? He remained in
Salzburg for nearly two years longer. He was now twenty,
a grown young man. His portrait, painted in 1777, showing
him wearing the star-shaped order of the Golden Spur which
the Pope had conferred on him, also clearly reveals the sense
of frustration from which he was suffering; he resembles
Leopold much more closely in this picture than in those
painted at later dates; even to the pessimistic expression of the
eyes and the sad set of the tightly-closed lips. During the past
few years he had continued to teach and to compose and to
while away the time with a few innocuous flirtations with local
young ladies. Yet his output during that time includes some of
his loveliest instrumental music.

The year after the Munich production of his opera, in September 1776, he had written a sorrowful letter to his old friend
and teacher, Padre Martini, in Bologna: 'I live in a country
where music leads a struggling existence . . . As for the theatre,
we are in a bad way for lack of singers . . . meanwhile I am
amusing myself by writing chamber music, and music for the
church.' He enclosed one of his motets with this letter. Padre
Martini replied three months later, very charmingly, that this
motet had 'all the qualities which modern music demands, good
harmony, rich modulation, etc.', but his letter contained no practical suggestions for employment, either in Italy or elsewhere.

In spite of his former difficulties—even with von Schratten-bach—in obtaining such frequent leaves from duty, Leopold made another attempt to do so in March 1777. Colloredo simply ignored it. His second request, in June, was curtly refused. From now on he was obliged to settle down in Salzburg, except for occasional trips to Munich and Vienna. In Wolfgang's case the Archbishop's attitude was even more irritating, for, after giving his more or less half-hearted consent to his absence on the grounds that he 'as only a half-time servant, anyway, could travel alone', he withdrew even that concession.

Colloredo did not, in fact, antagonize only the Mozarts. The people of his diocese almost unanimously loathed him; he also quarrelled with the Cathedral chapter. Historically, he holds a somewhat analogous position to that of Pontius Pilate, a mediocre Roman administrator who was unlucky enough to preside at the trial of Jesus, and thus assured himself of lasting notoriety. Colloredo would similarly have been ignored by posterity had his harshness been directed merely against Leopold Mozart, his cantankerous little assistant-conductor, and his colleagues. But the fact that the Vice-Kapellmeister's son, Wolfgang, happened to be a genius, raised their quarrel to an historical level.

One can imagine the arguments and the heart-searchings that took place during those miserable years in the house in the Makartplatz where the Mozart family lived; the atmosphere of secrecy, almost of conspiracy, in which they discussed their predicaments, for they felt themselves surrounded by enemies and spies. Leopold was undoubtedly on Wolfgang's side in this struggle. But to let him set out alone in search of a more congenial environment must have been cruelly hard for him. Nor was his reluctance due solely to his personal disappointment. To him his son, now in his twenty-second year, was still little more than a child, an irresponsible, even flighty youth, too fond by far of fun and games, parties, flirtations, and even drinking. He had little sense of monetary values, was easily led away by small kindnesses shown him or, worse, by mere flattery. He was gregarious, incautious, and when travelling, unsuspicious of the possibly evil intentions of his fellow-travellers. He meant well, no doubt, but if his heart was in the

right place there often seemed to his father to be a small
screw loose in his head.

It probably never occurred to Leopold that if Wolfgang
had still not grown up, this was largely due to the life he had
led hitherto—day and night under the tutelage of his fond but
dogmatic, suspicious and stern parent. But now Wolfgang
was in revolt, threatening to resign, to challenge authority—
his father's as well as Colloredo's—and to break away once and
for all. Leopold was shrewd enough to realize that he was in
earnest. Without sharing his son's confidence in the glorious
career that awaited him once he was free of Salzburg, he yet
felt that at least the boy must be given the chance of going
in search of it. But, and here Leopold was adamant, not alone.
If necessity chained his father to their tyrant's service, then his
mother would have to accompany him.

This decision must have brought a secret pang of pleasure
to Mama Mozart. Since the days of the children's early tours,
she, the least distinguished member of the family, had had to
enjoy Wolfgang's triumphs from a distance. Leopold's letters
from Italy and later from Vienna frequently allude to the
longings she had expressed to be with him and Wolfgang, and
he explained in detail why these could not be gratified, chiefly
on the grounds of the extra expense that would have been
incurred had he taken her along as well. Yet it was from his
mother and not from his father that Wolfgang had inherited
his natural gaiety, love of pleasure and distractions. So that
now, when unavoidable circumstances forced Leopold to send
his wife on Wolfgang's next journey with him, the good lady
must have been delighted, and, presumably no premonitions
of tragedy crossed her optimistic mind.

But first Wolfgang had to gain his release from service to
the Archbishop. The letter he wrote to him bears the clearest
marks of Leopold's authorship. Although it is formally respect-
ful enough—as indeed it would have had to be—the style
manages to blend smugness and humility in an uneasy
mixture:

Salzburg, August 1st, 1777

Your Grace, Most Worthy Prince of the Holy Roman
Empire!

I will not presume to trouble Your Grace with a full description of our unhappy circumstances, which my father has set forth most accurately in his very humble petition which was handed to you on March 14th, 1777. As, however, your most gracious decision was never conveyed to him, my father intended last June once more most respectfully to beg Your Grace to allow us to travel for a few months in order to enable us to make some money; and he would have done so, if you had not given orders that in view of the imminent visit of His Majesty the Emperor your orchestra should practise various works with a view to their performance. Later my father again applied for leave of absence, which Your Grace refused to grant, though you permitted me, who am in any case only a half-time servant, to travel alone. Our situation is pressing and my father has therefore decided to let me go alone. But to this course also Your Grace has been pleased to raise certain objections. Most Gracious Prince and Lord! Parents endeavour to place their children in a position to earn their own bread; and in this they follow alike their own interest and that of the State. The greater the talents which children have received from God, the more are they bound to use them for the improvement of their own and their parents' circumstances, so that they may at the same time assist them and take thought for their own future progress. The Gospel teaches us to use our talents in this way. My conscience tells me that I owe it to God to be grateful to my father, who has spent his time unwearyingly upon my education, so that I may lighten his burden, look after myself and later on be able to support my sister. For I should be sorry to think that she should have to spend so many hours at the harpsichord and not be able to make good use of her training.

Your Grace will therefore be so good as to allow me to ask you most humbly for my discharge, of which I should like to take advantage before the autumn, so that I may not be obliged to face the bad weather of the ensuing months of winter. Your Grace will not misunderstand this petition, seeing that when I asked you for permission to travel to Vienna three years ago, you graciously declared that I had nothing to hope for in Salzburg and would do better to seek my fortune elsewhere. I thank Your Grace for all the favours I have received from you and, in the hope of being able to serve you later on with greater success, I am,

your most humble and obedient servant
WOLFGANG AMADÉ MOZART

If Mozart rarely penned a musical phrase that could have been bettered, the same can hardly be said for this missive. One can almost see his tongue protruding from his cheek as he copied it out. Small wonder, then, that Colloredo, who was no fool, however heartless he may have been, forwarded this letter to his Court Chamberlain, who was to communicate his decision to its writer, with the following sarcastic and grimly amused comment: 'In the name of the Gospel, father and son have my permission to seek their fortune elsewhere.' He did not, however, show any personal vindictiveness towards Leopold and retained him in his service.

2

It had been decided that Wolfgang should make Paris his objective, travelling there in slow stages by way of south and west Germany. It is not difficult to imagine in what high spirits Mozart left, with his mother, on 23 September 1777. For not only was he at last free of Salzburg (in the determined conviction, in spite of the ending to his letter to the Archbishop, 'hoping to serve him with greater success in the future' never to return to work there again) but for the first time in his life he was no longer under Leopold's 'management'—either musical or personal.

The tour began at Augsburg, where Leopold was born, and where he had a brother and a niece, Maria Anna Thekla Mozart. She was a chubby, jolly, probably rather naughty girl, and at once started a violent flirtation with her brilliant young cousin. Neither they themselves nor their parents ever took it very seriously, not nearly so seriously at all events as some of Mozart's later, romantically-minded admirers. For after he had left Augsburg the two of them had a light-hearted and flippant correspondence. The letters Wolfgang then wrote to his 'Bäserl' (diminutive of 'Base', German for cousin) when published for the first time unexpurgated in 1938, caused more than slight consternation. For they contain certain very coarse scatological jokes and allusions, which were taken for granted in the eighteenth century and were also currently used by the whole Mozart family—including Mama—in their letters to one another. Scatological jokes, 'lavatory jokes' as we would say today, were quite usual in the eighteenth century. One of the more amusing of them is the remark attributed to Handel, on first hearing the bassoon: 'Praise be to God it hath no smell.' In the twentieth century we are most of us far less squeamish in these matters than our ancestors of the late nineteenth.

Humour and especially dirty humour is often, as Freud taught us, a psychological defence mechanism. In the days when plumbing as we now know it either did not exist or was of the most primitive kind, such jokes may have been a relief for having daily to endure unpleasant sights and smells. Moreover, a delight in trivial humour, even of a coarse character, is not nearly so uncommon in great creative artists as their more sentimental and romantic devotees might suppose. The more intense the creative work, the more exhausted its creator's mind is likely to be after having achieved it, or even during the process of doing so. Absurdities of all kinds bring welcome relaxation. The great performer is frequently by his very nature an extrovert and an exhibitionist. Mozart undoubtedly was one.

He also had an exuberant musical humour. This occasionally led him to indiscreet lengths, even in church, at the organ, as we shall shortly see. But it was a mere counterfoil to his very deep seriousness. And even in Augsburg, at the beginning of this tour, he by no means spent all his time merely amusing himself. During his stay there he visited the clavier-maker Stein, and was thrilled by the forte-pianos this excellent craftsman was turning out. He sent his father a long and detailed description of them and they remained his favourite instruments for his concert performances. They were the most efficient of their time, although not nearly so powerful as the modern instruments in use today. In spite, however, of his enthusiasm for Stein's craftmanship, Mozart astonished him when he told him that 'I should very much like to play on his organ, as that instrument was my passion, he was greatly surprised and said: "What? A man like you, so fine a piano-player, wants to play on an instrument which has no douceur, no expression, no piano, no forte, but is always the same?" "That does not matter," I replied, "In my eyes and ears the organ is the king of instruments."'

And as soon as he reached Mannheim, Mozart proclaimed this passion by playing on the organs in several churches. It was on one of these occasions that his sense of humour ran away with him. In spite of the fact that he hoped to obtain a post as organist in that city, when trying out the organ in the private chapel of the Elector, Karl Theodor, during the celebration of the Mass, he let himself go to the extent of improvizing a cadenza at the end of the Gloria and inventing a fugue on the theme of the Sanctus. This may have been a good example of virtuosity, but hardly of manners.

Leopold became more and more worried as he received Wolfgang's exuberant letters. It was clear that in addition to his other peccadilloes, he and his mother were enjoying the good Rhine wine somewhat frequently and copiously—Wolfgang especially—and some of those letters, written very hastily and late at night, filled with doggerel, rigmarole, and nonsense of all kinds, bear witness to its effects. Leopold's replies of enormous length were filled with admonitions, instructions, criticisms, and heavily underlined passages counselling wisdom, prudence, and giving his son detailed directions regarding his social and professional behaviour.

Yet here again Wolfgang was by no means merely frivolous. The Elector was a great musical patron and his orchestra was large, superbly rehearsed, and rightly famous throughout Germany. In addition to splendid string-players, it contained a very fine woodwind section, including clarinets. Mozart had already heard and even composed some pieces for this latter instrument before his visit to Mannheim. But now he realized its delightful potentialities more clearly than before and was to put it to enchanting use in his later works, both in his symphonies and in the exquisite concerto and quintet he wrote for it. A whole number of composers—then celebrated but now remembered only by musicologists for the influence their works had on Mozart's development—were constantly writing new symphonies for this orchestra in the modern German style. But there was so much competition that Wolfgang had to work terribly hard to pay his and his mother's expenses, mainly by giving lessons. At the same time he was busily composing. His mother wrote to his father:

Mannheim January 3-4, 1778

Wolfgang has not come home yet. Whether he will get back in time to add a few lines I really don't know. He has a lot of composing to do, time simply flies, and he has, as it were, to steal it . . . when he must go to one place for his meals, to another to compose and give lessons, and to yet another when he wants to sleep . . .

They had arrived in Mannheim in November 1777, and there was still no prospect of Mozart receiving any sort of permanent post. He was giving lessons to the illegitimate children of the Elector, and had hopes of further favours. But Karl Theodor had more important things on his mind. The Elector of Bavaria died on 30 December, and Karl Theodor, after having himself proclaimed in Mannheim as his successor, immediately departed for Munich to assume the Electorship, to which he had an hereditary claim. This was supported by the Austrian Emperor, Joseph II, but contested by Frederick the Great of Prussia. Their quarrel led to the War of the Bavarian Succession, which broke out in the following year. The letters exchanged between Leopold and his wife and son express their anxiety over these political events. However, they suffered no personal nor direct ill consequences from them. And ultimately Wolfgang was to benefit very greatly from the removal of the Mannheim Court—complete with orchestra and leading singers—to Munich.

It was obvious, however, that no useful purpose could be served by his lingering on in Mannheim during the first two months of 1778. Leopold was making plans for his wife's return to Salzburg, and Wolfgang's journey to Paris. As their letters took the best part of a week to reach the recipients, many of them crossed, and the delays were a further cause of irritation to Leopold. On 29 January 1778, he sent Wolfgang another of his enormous screeds, which contained a warning: 'You should refrain from all familiarity with young Frenchmen, and even more so with the women, who are always on the lookout for strangers to keep them, who run after young people of talent in an astonishing way in order to get at their money, draw them into their net or even land them as husband . . . Any such calamity would be the death of me!'

But, alas, what appeared to Leopold to be such a calamity

had already occurred in Mannheim. His dutiful son announced it to him in a letter written on 4 February 1778, which, when his infuriated parent read it, must have burst like a bombshell before his eyes. For Wolfgang had fallen in love and, as if to confirm his father's worst premonitions, with the most unsuitable young person imaginable.

Her name was Aloysia Weber. She was only fifteen years old, but had an exquisite voice and was already an accomplished singer. She was the daughter of Fridolin Weber, a miserable hack, theatrical prompter, and musical copyist, who had three other growing girls to support as well—Josefa, Constanze and Sophie.

The first news Wolfgang gave his father of this undesirable connection was in a letter of 17 January, in which he described the distressing plight of this 'thoroughly honest German', obliged to bring up his family on a miserable pittance. He was already ecstatic about Aloysia's talents. He shortly afterwards left Mannheim for a week with the Webers, to perform at the castle of the Princess of Weilburg, a short distance away from the town. A good time was undoubtedly had by all, but without much financial profit.

Leopold's feelings can be better imagined than described, when in his letter of 4 February, Wolfgang proposed throwing the whole Paris project overboard and going off to Italy with the Weber family, in order to write operas for Aloysia, in which she would captivate that country's capricious public! The letter is quite touching, no more foolish than that of any youth suffering from a severe attack of calf-love. But Leopold had been having to borrow money to send to his wife and son —who was now twenty-two—he was running into debt in order to support them at a distance, so that this crazy project of Wolfgang's was really too much! Nor was his alarm allayed by receiving at the same time a letter from his wife, who was equally worried. She, too, thoroughly disapproved of the Webers, complained that Wolfgang would not listen to her, and suggested to her husband that she should accompany him to Paris. She ended her short but dramatic note: 'I am writing this quite secretly, while he is at dinner, and I shall close, for I do not want to be caught.'

Chapter VI

PARIS, 1778

LEOPOLD's lamentations and comminations were of almost Biblical fervour. 'Your wild letter . . . which almost killed me' elicited a reply running to some two thousand five hundred words. He fulminated, he argued, he reproached, he even cosseted. Nothing was forgiven or forgotten. 'The Prince's (the Archbishop's) conduct can only bend me, but yours can crush me . . .' Even a reference to the famous 'Next to God comes Papa' was included in order to soften his wayward son's heart. Yet it was also an admirable letter, for it was abundantly clear that even now Leopold had not lost faith in Wolfgang's genius, and was, in fact, fighting and struggling against the foolish young man in its interest. 'What a responsibility! And what a shame if such a great genius were to founder!'

This epistle, of 23 February 1778, was immediately followed by another one, almost as long, written during the 25th to 26th. In this one he even generously said that he would do his best for Mlle Weber. The reason is fairly obvious, for he would gladly have helped her on her way to Italy or even further, to remove his son, whose own objective was to be Paris, from her toils.

Wolfgang's capitulation to his father's commands and appeals was immediate. For although he was still seeing Aloysia and had even written another wonderful aria for her, there was now no more talk of taking her to Italy. He ended his letter of 28 February, which was also of considerable length:

> Remember that you have a son who has never, knowingly, forgotten his filial duty to you, who will endeavour to become more and more worthy of so good a father and who will remain unchangingly your most obedient
>
> WOLFGANG MOZART

He consoled himself by writing another very long, lighthearted, and nonsensical letter to his little cousin in Augsburg.

Preparations for the Paris visit were now going forward. Leopold had received an amiable letter from a former friend and patron there, Baron Friedrich Melchior Grimm, offering to put up Wolfgang and his mother. They arrived in Paris on 24 March 1778, after an intensely boring journey which had taken nine and a half days. In his very first letter Wolfgang wrote to his father at some length how kindly and affectionately the Webers had parted from him—'Forgive me, but my eyes fill with tears when I recall the scene.'

In this and subsequent references to them in his letters home, he wrote to his father, not defiantly, but rather as if he still hoped to persuade him of the merits of this unfortunate family, of whom the head, Fridolin Weber, had, from his own point of view most unwisely, informed Frau Mozart that her son was their best friend and benefactor. And in considering Wolfgang's behaviour during the following months, both personally and professionally, the importance of the fact that he was at that time deeply in love with Aloysia Weber has often been overlooked.

At his father's command he had gone to Paris to make a career there, but it was as if he felt in advance that he would fail to do so. One might almost suggest that he was determined on failure, for he had not the slightest wish to settle in Paris; his heart was in Mannheim with Aloysia, and crazy as had been his plan to take her to Italy, this was and remained his dream.

Furthermore, although Leopold had sent Wolfgang to Paris hoping that as a fully-fledged composer and performer he would repeat his childhood's sensational success there, he himself had never liked the French nor admired their culture. Wolfgang was now twenty-two but still intellectually dominated by his father. It is only necessary to compare Leopold's priggishly disapproving letters to Hagenauer from Paris and Versailles in 1764 with those Wolfgang was now writing home to see how deeply his father's antipathy to the French and all their works had sunk into his own mind.

From the moment of his arrival he found France and Frenchmen—Frenchwomen, too—antipathetic, uncongenial and depressing. He complained of the enormous distances he had to travel to make professional or social calls; the roads were filthy and carriages like everything else, extremely expensive. So he made as few visits as possible. To top his annoyance, the aristocracy surpassed itself in insolence. He described with justified fury how he called on one grand lady, who, after having kept him waiting for ages in an ice-cold room, invited him to play the harpsichord, whilst she herself sat at her drawing-board surrounded by male admirers, none of them paying any attention to the music. Very shortly after his arrival Mozart composed an exquisite concerto for flute and harp (K. 299) for the Duc de Guines and his daughter, to whom he also gave lessons. They went off to the country some months later, without troubling to pay him for either. M. Jean Le Gros, the director of the Concert Spirituel, accepted a sinfonia concertante, but instead of sending it to the copyist forgot all about it. Wolfgang felt himself surrounded by ene-mies, hemmed in by intrigues and jealous rivals, and in the absence of Leopold, who in the past had always fought such battles on his behalf—and had clearly enjoyed doing so—was helpless to cope with his real or imaginary difficulties. He hoped to get a commission to write an opera, although in competition with the fashionable composers then in vogue, he had little chance of it. Moreover, he thought the French lan-guage musically detestable and was equally contemptuous of the native singers. His only success in this sphere was the composition of some charming but light ballet music, appro-priately entitled *Les petits riens* (K. App. 10).

He had one outstanding success, however. This was with his Symphony (K. 297) which is known nowadays as the 'Paris', which he wrote for the Concert Spirituel. But even in describ-ing this work to Leopold, he wrote in a thoroughly bad temper: 'I cannot say whether it will be popular—and, to tell the truth, I care very little, for who will not like it? I can answer for its pleasing the few intelligent French people who may be there—and as for the stupid ones, I shall not consider it a great mis-fortune if they are not pleased.'

Nor was Frau Mozart having a very happy time. Wolfgang was out nearly all day as there was no harpsichord in their lodgings, so that he went to Le Gros's to use one there. In her letters the good lady gives her husband details of the bad food: 'a slab of calf's foot in some dirty sauce', and 'everything here is half as dear again as it was the last time we were here twelve years ago'. Nevertheless, she tried to keep cheerful and sent her daughter an amusing description of the fashions of the day: 'The "mode" here is to wear no ear-rings, nothing round your neck, no jewelled pins in your hair, in fact, no sparkling jewels, either real or imitation. The frisure they wear is extraordinarily high, not a heart-shaped toupee, but the same height all round, more than a foot. The cap, which is even higher than the toupee, is worn on top, and behind is the plait or chignon which is worn right down low into the neck with lots of curls on either side. The toupee, however, consists entirely of crepe, not of smooth hair. They have been wearing this frisure even higher, so that at one time the roofs of the carriages had to be raised, because no woman could sit upright in them. But they have now lowered them again.'

She wrote also that all the women carried walking-sticks 'because it is very slippery here underfoot, particularly after the rain'. But Frau Mozart, in her letter to her husband on 29 May 1778, also discussed the political situation, and the threatened war.

Wolfgang as well as his mother frequently alluded to this situation and urged Leopold, in the event of the war—which broke out at the end of the following July—endangering Salzburg, to join them in Paris, as it was the safest place to be.

Leopold, with his usual interest in scientific matters, had asked his wife for some information about the lightning conductor, or lightning rod, which had been invented by the great American philosopher, scientist and statesman, Benjamin Franklin. Frau Mozart replied: 'As for the lightning conductor I can't find out what people here think about it, as I don't know the language. But I have not seen any. In Mannheim, however, it cropped up once in conversation. They don't think much of it there, for they say that it attracts storms, when there would otherwise be none at all, and that where there are many conductors, the storm settles in that particular spot until everything is smashed to pieces and all the crops destroyed. It is far better to let nature take its course than to force it. For God can find anybody he wants to and no lightning conductor can save him.'

However unscientific Frau Mozart or her friends may have been with regard to the lightning conductor, her final sentence in this letter of 12 June 1778, the last she was to write to her devoted husband, was sadly prophetic. For on 3 July God sought her out, so far from her family and her home, in a strange country, among people whose language she could not speak, and she died.

She had apparently been unwell for some time previously. Naturally enough, she had not wanted to call in a French doctor, but by the time a German one was found, it was too late to save her. In view of the current treatment for an intestinal infection, which seems to have been the cause of her death, her case must have been pretty hopeless from the start. Bleeding and a rhubarb powder in wine! Even Wolfgang in his ignorance remonstrated with the doctor, but to no purpose.

His mother's death was of course a shattering blow to him. 'As long as I live I shall never forget it. You know that I had never seen anyone die, although I had often wished to. How cruel that my first experience should be the death of my mother!' He was appalled, as well, at having to break the news to his father. So on the night of 3 July, when she was already dead, he wrote Leopold, telling him of her grave illness, preparing him for the blow, and he also wrote at the same time to the family's best friend, the Abbé Bullinger, giving him the true facts and asking him to break them as gently as possible to his father. He wrote again to his father on 9 and 31 July, giving him fuller details of his mother's death.

All these very long letters also contained references to his current work and plans. This might seem surprising to those who find it difficult to understand the different attitudes towards death of the eighteenth and twentieth centuries. Two hundred years ago human life was commonly short and precarious. But for that very reason religious belief was deeply fatalistic and strong. Death of a loved one was God's will. It aroused legitimate grief but little resentment. In his letters to his father Wolfgang describes with obvious sincerity how passionately he prayed for his mother's life, and also for fortitude to bear the blow if this prayer were not granted. And once she was dead, he accepted the situation completely, as, indeed, did Leopold. It may seem callous to us, but life in the eighteenth century was lived on a much ruder level than life in the twentieth. Possibly neither of them was typical of their period in this respect; possibly another family might have reacted differently. The Mozarts undoubtedly had unusual powers of adaptation, to both good and bad fortune. And as they had more than their share of the latter, that may have been a very good thing in their case. Basta!—(enough)—Leopold would say and write at the end of a sentence, when clearly nothing more could be done or hoped for. *Basta!* An expression similar in emotional content to the Russian *Nitchevo* —a verbal shrug of the shoulders as it were, and a 'now let us get on with the next business'.

Leopold, in his replies to Wolfgang regarding the death of the wife whom he had deeply loved—'I write with tears in my eyes, but in complete submission to the will of God'—proceeds in his next letter to give his son advice and instructions as to returning home 'your dear Mamma's *clothes and linen—her watch—her ring and her other jewelry*' all heavily underlined, and which he will have to pack carefully in some chest or box, together with several musical scores.

In spite of his very long letters on the subject, his filial and religious piety, Wolfgang's grief for his mother was conventional rather than emotional. The truth is that his heart was not in Paris but in Mannheim. At the end of May he had written to his father: 'I am tolerably well, thank God, but I often wonder whether life is worth living—I am neither hot nor cold—and don't find much pleasure in anything'—a sentence and a condition typical of any young man hopelessly in love. One need merely compare his letters to his father on his mother's death to those written at the end of July to Fridolin and Aloysia Weber to see what a difference there was between his conventional expressions of grief and his natural feelings. There is ample evidence that although he was in love with Weber's daughter, Wolfgang was also genuinely attached to her insignificant father. His relationship with Fridolin was a kind of inversion of his natural relationship with his own father. Whereas the latter had always been his best but sternest and most critical friend, Fridolin appeared to him to be as persecuted and as struggling as he himself was, and even more worthily in need of help and protection. There was almost nothing he would not have done to help him and, of course, his family, and he even suggested—though he must have known how utterly impracticable this was—that they should all join him in Paris. 'But sad as my present position is, I am infinitely more disappointed to think that I am not able to serve you', and there is not the slightest doubt that he really believed and meant it.

One cannot help sympathizing with the annoyance Leopold felt when he received another long letter from Wolfgang, written on 31 July, which began with a detailed description of his poor mother's illness and medical maltreatment, but ended with another passionate plea for help to the Webers: 'If only I could help them! Dearest father! I commend them to you with all my heart. If only they could enjoy an income of a thousand gulden (about £100) even for a few years!' Leopold cannot be blamed at all for now losing his temper with his son, and sending him a brutally blunt reply, in which he more or less accused him and 'those Webers' of having been responsible for his mother's death. He revealed to him for the first time how Frau Mozart had secretly written to her husband from Mannheim about Wolfgang's attachment to them; how it was she who had suggested going on to Paris with him to rescue him from them, and that 'if your mother had returned home from Mannheim, she would not have died. But as Divine Providence had fixed the hour of her death for July 3rd, she had to leave home with you and, owing to your new friendship, her return had to be abandoned'.

He continued by pointing out, quoting and italicizing, all the absurdities his son had written about them, refuting them one by one, blowing an icy gust of common sense on all Wolfgang's romantic dreams.

Mozart had now been in Paris for four months and his prospects of success there were dwindling instead of mounting. Baron von Grimm, in whose house he was living since his mother's death, sent Leopold very discouraging reports of him, of his reluctance to take the necessary trouble to establish himself there socially and professionally. He also told Wolfgang himself, quite candidly, that he saw no hope for him there at all. Mozart's reluctance to settle in France emerged very clearly in his letter to Leopold of 14 May 1778, in which he told him rather casually, right at the end, that he was offered the post of organist at Versailles: 'The salary is 2,000 livres a year, but I should have to spend six months at Versailles and the other six in Paris, or wherever I like. I do not think that I shall accept it . . . After all, 2,000 livres is not such a big sum.'

2

In Salzburg, meanwhile, a reorganization of the Prince's
musical staff was in progress. A new conductor-in-chief was
being sought for his orchestra. Leopold thought himself entitled to the post, but, in spite of endless machinations and intrigues, failed to get it. His debts were pressing and, honourable
man that he was, the thought of them weighed upon him like
a constant nightmare. He saw himself having to go on keeping
himself, Nannerl, and probably his impecunious son, as well,
by hack-work and teaching, and he was by now getting on for
sixty. There was no help for it; Wolfgang would have to come
home and get himself re-appointed to the Archbishop's service.
In his letters he put matters as tactfully as he could. Colloredo
needed an organist and assistant conductor, and if this meant
playing a violin in his orchestra, well, the Archbishop himself
did so on occasions, for his own amusement, along with his
professional and amateur underlings, so there was no disgrace
attached to doing the same. Colloredo was not unwilling to
receive young Mozart back into his service; he knew he could
hardly get a better musician more cheaply, and there was
probably a grain of satisfied malice in his benevolent reception
of Leopold's overtures. At the end of August the latter had
everything laid on, to his own satisfaction, if not to Wolfgang's.
'Not only has the Archbishop agreed to everything, both for
me and for you (you are to have five hundred gulden) but he
has even apologized for not being able at the present moment
to appoint you Kapellmeister; you are, however, to take my
place if I am tired or indisposed; and he mentioned that he had
always intended that you should have a better salary, etc.
. . . The Archbishop has declared that he will give you leave to
travel where you like for the purpose of composing an opera.
To excuse himself for having refused us leave last year, he said
that he could not tolerate people going about the world beg-
ging. In Salzburg you will be midway between Munich,
Vienna and Italy . . . My next letter will tell you that you are
to leave.'

This reference to Italy and Munich was an artful one. For
together with the rest of the Elector's musical personnel, the
Webers had gone to Munich, and referring to this in a later
letter Leopold remarked dourly: 'Your desire that the Webers

should have a thousand gulden a year has been fulfilled, for a letter from Munich of September 15th informs me that Count Seeau has engaged Mlle Weber for the German theatre at six hundred gulden. So if you add her father's four hundred, they will have a thousand.'

That poor fish, Wolfgang, was now hooked. In any case he was at heart thankful to leave that detestable city, Paris, and probably—even apart from his yearning for the Webers—thoroughly homesick. He tried to save face by claiming that had he remained in Paris a little longer, he would have made good there. The thought of Salzburg was still hateful to him, and in any case there was no doubt that it was an ignominious retreat, a bitter ending to the high hopes of fortune and celebrity with which he had set out. Once more he would be under the paternal roof and thumb, would have to assume the livery of servitude. He drew out his return journey as long as he possibly could, travelling via Mannheim, Nancy, Strassburg and Munich. There a dreadful shock awaited him. Aloysia did not love him.

Whether she had ever reciprocated his passion is indeed questionable. She was an excellent, ambitious singer, with a lovely voice. In Mannheim her adorer had written arias for her and had taken the greatest trouble to train and teach her. There is nothing to her discredit in having accepted his professional help and even possibly at that time encouraged his advances, though with due maidenly reserve. She was only fifteen at the time, little more than a child. Her unprosperous parent had three other daughters to support, and no doubt would gladly have accepted Mozart as a son-in-law and provider.

Many years later, when she was an elderly woman, Aloysia herself gave the following account to Mary Novello: 'She told me Mozart always loved her until the day of his death, which to speak candidly she fears has occasioned a slight jealousy on the part of her sister. I asked her why she refused him, she could not tell, the fathers were both agreed (*sic*) but she could not love him at that time, she was not capable of appreciating his talent and his amiable character, but afterwards she much regretted it.'

Aloysia was of course remembering the mature Mozart, who

by that time had become an acknowledged celebrity, and was anxious to perpetuate the legend of their romance. There is no evidence at all that after his marriage to Constanze, Wolfgang still loved her sister. And as for the alleged agreement of their two fathers, this statement was either due to a lapse of memory on Aloysia's part, or pure romancing.

What is certain is Mozart's devoted attachment, from the moment of his first meeting with them, until he died, to the entire Weber family. And now, writing to his father from Munich on 29 December, he told him that he could only weep, that his heart was full of tears, and asked him to reply care of the Poste Restante, because he was staying with the Webers. Nor did Aloysia's refusal, although it hurt him so deeply, either break off his connection with the family, or prevent him from sending for his Bäserl to join him and console him in Munich a week later. He even wrote to Leopold, asking his permission to bring her to Salzburg with him. This elicited the acid rejoinder that 'if my niece wants to honour me with a visit, *she can follow on the 20th* (of January 1779) *by the mail coach*'.

Leopold was by now in a frenzy over Wolfgang's procrastinations and delays in returning home. He feared that Colloredo would lose patience and cancel his son's appointment. It was useless for Wolfgang to reply that 'I cannot bear Salzburg or its inhabitants . . . Their language—their manners are quite intolerable to me'. He returned home in the middle of January, his bid for freedom having ended, 'not with a bang but a whimper':

Salzburg, January 1779

Your Grace,
Most Worthy Prince of the Holy Roman Empire!
Most Gracious Prince and Lord!

After the decease of Cajetan Adlgasser Your Grace was so good as to take me into your service. I therefore humbly beseech you to grant me a certificate of my appointment as Court Organist.

I remain,

Your Grace's most humble and obedient servant,
Wolfgang Amadé Mozart

Chapter VII

REBELLION

ONE of Wolfgang's grievances against Salzburg was that there was no opera company there. Nevertheless, in his boredom after his obligatory return he tried to distract himself by writing an opera that might be performed by local amateurs. It was entitled *Zaïde*, and the libretto was by the Mozart's old family friend, Schachtner, who had known Wolfgang ever since he was born. He never finished it, because the work was interrupted by more exciting operatic activities.

Salzburg's theatrical life was brightened for a short time when a touring company arrived there directed by Emanuel Schikaneder. One of the plays in his repertoire was called *Thamos, King of Egypt*, to which Mozart had already composed some incidental music after his return from Italy in 1773. At Schikaneder's invitation, Mozart now re-wrote this. When produced by Schikaneder the play was a failure. But their friendship formed at this time was to endure, and led many years later to the composition and triumphant success of Mozart's last and greatest German opera, *The Magic Flute*.

He was now twenty-four and the prospect of life in Salzburg seemed more disheartening than ever. But just at this depressing moment his friends in Munich were able to give him the chance he had been longing for—another commission, to compose a full-length opera seria for the carnival of 1781. Mozart would have liked it to be a gay opera buffa, but the libretto, provided by the Archbishop's chaplain, the Abbé Varesco, was a conventionally tragic one, modelled on the Greek themes then fashionable, in imitation of those of Metastasio. It was entitled *Idomeneo*.

To Wolfgang's even greater joy he was also able to take advantage of Colloredo's promise to allow him to travel for the purpose of composing an opera. He arrived in Munich early in November in order to write the music in close touch with the company that was to sing it. His librettist remained in Salzburg and Leopold acted as intermediary between them. Wolfgang's letters to his father were full of details of his work. Varesco's libretto was clumsy, unwieldy, far too long, yet like better dramatists he opposed all cuts and alterations. Mozart, whose musical reputation was at stake, nevertheless unhesitatingly made certain cuts and changes in it, conceding that to pacify its author it could be published in full.

The story tells how Idomeneo, King of Crete, returns home from the Trojan war after an absence of twenty years. Approaching harbour his fleet is menaced by a terrific storm, whereupon the king vows that if spared, he will sacrifice to the Sea God the first human being he encounters ashore. This person is, of course, his son, Idamante, now grown up, and when the king becomes aware of their relationship he tries to evade his oath by sending the young man to accompany a lady refugee, Electra (in love with him) back to her home. Idamante himself is in love with another maiden, Ilia, a Trojan captive. The cheated sea-god sends a monster to destroy Idomeneo and his people. Idamante kills this creature and just as he himself is, nevertheless, about to be sacrificed—his father having been compelled by his subjects to disclose his rash vow and the name of the victim—the voice of an oracle is heard announcing that Idomeneo is to abdicate in his son's favour. The gods and the people are appeased and all ends well.

Although the libretto appeals more to the modern sense of humour than to awe of prophecies and oracles as it was meant to do, the music of this opera is a different matter. Mozart of course took the subject seriously and to good purpose. The score contains some of his noblest music and, partly modelled on the style of Gluck, whose works he had heard in Paris, some superb choruses. For a long time it was almost totally neglected. But its beauty and nobility has caused *Idomeneo* to be resurrected more and more frequently in recent years. The absurdities of the plot are overlooked as one listens to the impressive arias and ensembles, and, above all, the accompanied recitatives.

On its first performance in Munich the work had a great success. Leopold and Nannerl came over from Salzburg to hear it. But there was one notable absentee—the Archbishop, who in the meantime had left Salzburg for Vienna. As he planned to remain there during the summer he had taken a large staff with him, including his leading court musicians. He required the attendance of young Mozart there as well, in order that he might conduct or play the clavier at the concerts with which the Archbishop was planning to entertain his aristocratic friends. After the successful production of *Idomeneo* Wolfgang had been wholeheartedly enjoying the gaieties of the Munich carnival. But his pleasures were abruptly brought to an end when, at the beginning of March 1781, he was commanded by his Prince to join his household in Vienna forthwith.

On arrival, Mozart was lodged and boarded exactly like his two colleagues, Gaetano Brunetti, the principal violinist, and Ceccarelli, the singer. They were none of them especially signalled out for ignominious treatment. But if the other two musicians took their humble social status for granted, Mozart found it outrageous and intolerable: 'We lunch about twelve o'clock, unfortunately somewhat too early for me. Our party consists of two valets, that is, the body and soul attendants of His Worship, the contrôleur, Herr Zetti, the confectioner, the two cooks, Ceccarelli, Brunetti, and—my insignificant self! By the way, the two valets sit at the top of the table, but at least I have the honour of being placed above the cooks.'

His salary in the Archbishop's service was not five hundred gulden, as Leopold had written to him that it was to be, but four hundred and fifty. He was expected to play whenever and wherever his master wished, with no extra remuneration for doing so. He was, of course, also getting free lodging and board in the circumstances he so bitterly described in this letter to Leopold. He ends it with a threat: 'I shall go to the Archbishop and tell him with absolute frankness that if he will not allow me to earn anything, then he must pay me, for I cannot live at my own expense.'

But the Archbishop had not sent for his musicians in order that they should make their own fortunes whilst in his employment. Wolfgang was very soon invited to play at a concert at which he would not even have earned a fee, for it was in aid of charity: 'No virtuoso who has any love for his neighbour, refuses to give his services, if the society asks him to do so.

Besides, in this way he can win the favour both of the Emperor and of the public . . . I agreed at once, adding, however, that I must first obtain the consent of my Prince, which I had not the slightest doubt that he would give—as it was a matter of charity, or at any rate a good work, for which I would get no fee. *He would not permit me to take part.*' The Archbishop was, however, compelled to surrender on that occasion, not to Mozart's request, but to the expressed wish of the nobility. This cannot on any count have endeared his refractory employee to him. Mozart was already making plans to perform in Vienna and to meet the Emperor, when he was informed by Count Karl Arco, the Archbishop's Chamberlain, that he, together with the other musicians, was to return to Salzburg on 22 April:

> Vienne, ce 11 d'avril 1781
>
> . . . When I think that I must leave Vienna without bringing home *at least* a thousand gulden, my heart is sore indeed. So, for the sake of a malevolent Prince who plagues me every day and only pays me a lousy salary of four hundred gulden, I am to kick away a thousand . . .

His fury was increased by the fact that he had had to play at a concert for the Archbishop, for which he received a tip of four ducats when 'that very same evening we had this foul concert I was invited to Countess Thun's, but of course could not go; and who should be there but *the Emperor*!' Wolfgang was writing week by week to his father, imploring Leopold to give his paternal approval to his mutinous plans, pointing out that if he remained in Vienna he could and would make his fortune at last. An impresario called Gottlieb Stephanie had suggested giving him an opera libretto; he could give very profitable concerts and also lessons to the aristocracy. As an added inducement he even promised to send his father money.

It was quite clear that, come what might, he had resolved never to return to Salzburg and servitude. The situation had now gone far beyond Leopold's powers of remote control. His son was twenty-five years of age and for the first time wrote to him as man to man, although still respectfully and devotedly.

He was avoiding any direct approach to the Archbishop and

on one pretext or another—although not yet having openly
disobeyed his master's orders to leave—postponed his departure from Vienna from day to day. But the tension between
them was rising as rapidly as a spring tide and it finally over-
flowed on 9 May 1781, one of the most important dates in
Mozart's life, when their mutual antagonism exploded in a
great rip-roaring row. He wrote a detailed account of it to
Leopold on that very same date: 'I am still seething with rage!
. . . My patience has been so long tried that at last it has given
out. I am no longer so unfortunate as to be in Salzburg service.
To-day is a happy day for me.' A week previously he had been
ordered by a mere footman 'to clear out that very instant'.
He packed his trunk and went elsewhere, whilst again post-
poning his departure for Salzburg. On the ninth, he went to
take his leave, officially, from the Archbishop: 'Well, when I
entered the room, his first words were: *Archbishop:* "Well,
young fellow, when are you going off?" *I:* "I intended to
go to-night, but all the seats were already engaged." Then he
rushed full steam ahead, without pausing for breath—I was
the most dissolute fellow he knew—no one served him so badly
as I did—I had better leave to-day or else he would write
home and have my salary stopped. I couldn't get a word in
edgeways, for he blazed away like a fire. I listened to it all very
calmly. He lied to my face that my salary was five hundred
gulden, called me a scoundrel, a rascal, a vagabond . . . At last
my blood began to boil, I could no longer contain myself and
I said, "So Your Grace is not satisfied with me?" "What,
you dare to threaten me, you scoundrel? There is the door!
Look out, for I will have nothing more to do with such a
miserable wretch." At last I said: "Nor I with you!" "Well,
be off!" When leaving the room I said, "This is final. You
shall have it to-morrow in writing." '

As in his previous letters, when discussing the Archbishop
and their relations, Wolfgang wrote this one in the family
cipher that Leopold had invented for their more confidential
communications.

Had his father not sympathized with him it would be
surprising. But in view of his own position and his fear of
losing it owing to his son's troubles, he dared not take his side.
Leopold was now getting on for seventy. Marianne was an old

maid—thirty—and although they both gave lessons in Salzburg her father was faced with the prospect of having to provide for her. Wolfgang might do better for himself in Vienna, but Leopold was a life-long pessimist and, alas, as far as his son was concerned his pessimism was not unjustified. And there was another aspect to Wolfgang's plans which made it impossible for Leopold to accept the prospect of his remaining in Vienna with equanimity.

It was still necessary for Mozart to present his notice, in the form of a petition to be released from his service, to the Archbishop. Colloredo himself would have nothing more to do with him, and so he made three attempts to settle the matter with the Chamberlain, Count Arco. Leopold, whether to save his own skin or because he really had lost patience, had apparently written to Arco and, as the latter told Wolfgang during their second interview, had complained bitterly about his son. When told this, Mozart nevertheless remained adamant in his determination to resign his post. 'Upon which he said: "Believe me, you allow yourself to be far too easily dazzled in Vienna. A man's reputation here lasts a very short time . . ." "You are right, Count," I replied, "but . . . that this affair should have occurred in Vienna is the Archbishop's fault and not mine. If he knew how to treat people of talent it would never have happened. I am the best-tempered fellow in the world, Count Arco, provided that people are the same with me." "Well," he said, "the Archbishop considers you a dreadfully conceited person . . ." ' During this interview Count Arco seems to have been attempting an attitude of sweet reasonableness and reconciliation, and finding it quite useless, must have begun to lose patience to a considerable extent. He did not forward Mozart's petition to the Prince, so that Wolfgang was obliged again to apply in person for his discharge. Now the Chamberlain took a leaf from his master's book; abused the presumptuous young man as roundly, in equally insulting terms, and ended the interview summarily, by kicking him on the behind and throwing him out of the room.

The most poignant element in this scene was not the insult itself, which had undoubtedly been given under considerable provocation, but the profound cleavage between Mozart's consciousness of his own genius and its evaluation by his aristocratic persecutors. By the conventions of his day he was utterly prohibited from avenging himself. But that kick from the Count propelled him from youth into manhood. From that moment onwards he belonged to the new age—the age of Revolution, that was to wipe out the old feudal order and introduce the concepts of liberty, equality, and fraternity into the social and political worlds. 'It is the heart that ennobles a man' (he wrote to his father on 20 June 1781) 'and though I am no count, yet I have probably more honour in me than many a count.'

In 1783 a play was produced in Paris entitled *Le Mariage de Figaro*. Its author was Caron de Beaumarchais, and its hero was a writer who, in order to gain a living, had become barber and valet to an aristocratic Spaniard, Count Almaviva. Figaro's great monologue in this play begins: 'My lord Count, because you are a great aristocrat, you think yourself a great genius! . . . nobility, fortune, rank, influence, all that makes one so proud! What did you do to earn so many advantages? You gave yourself the trouble of being born and nothing more: for the rest, a rather commonplace person, whereas I, by Jove! lost in the common herd, have had to deploy a greater degree of thought and scheming than has been spent in the past hundred years in governing the whole of Spain.' There could hardly have been a composer better qualified both by genius and affinity to write *Le Nozze di Figaro*, the great opera based on this play, than Wolfgang Amadeus Mozart.

2

Leopold's anger with Wolfgang was due not only to his rebellion against Colloredo, but also to another and even more threatening situation that had arisen. In the first letter in which Wolfgang had informed him that the Archbishop's footman had ordered him to 'clear out that very instant', he had continued 'and old Madame Weber has been good enough to take me into her house, where I have a pretty room.' For Wolfgang had not lost touch with his old friends. His prediction in Mannheim days that Aloysia would make a great success as an opera singer was being fulfilled. In September 1779— whilst he himself was still living miserably in Salzburg—she had been engaged by the German opera company in Vienna.

Her father, poor Fridolin, had died shortly afterwards. Her mother had then moved with her four daughters to an apartment house known as the 'Auge Gottes' (God's Eye) and let out rooms in order to provide for them. Aloysia in the following year married Josef Lange, an actor who as such has no great claims on posterity. But he was, fortunately, also an excellent artist and in 1782 painted a portrait of Mozart which, although unfinished, is generally regarded as the best likeness of all.

Leopold continued as usual to write nagging, reproachful letters. Wolfgang replied to them with really amazing patience and gentleness, but with a new firmness. His decision to remain in Vienna was irrevocable. His father was still accusing him of being influenced by his passion for Aloysia. He refuted this contention in a most dignified manner, and with admirable candour: 'What you say about the Webers I do assure you is not true. I was a fool, I admit, about Aloysia Lange, but what does a man not do when he is in love? Indeed I loved her truly, and even now I feel that she is not a matter of indifference to me. It is therefore a good thing for me that her husband is a jealous fool and lets her go nowhere, so that I seldom have an opportunity of seeing her. Believe me when I say that old Madame Weber is a very obliging woman and that I cannot do enough for her in return for her kindness.' Old Madame Weber was quite a character. And Wolfgang could not have found a more congenial home. For she and her daughters, although passably respectable, belonged to the world of artists and had nothing in common with those intensely narrow-minded Catholic bourgeois small-town circles in which Leopold lived, and in which he had his moral as well as physical being.

Leopold had, in fact, always demanded the impossible of his son. He acknowledged his genius, yet he expected him to adjust himself to every petty lower middle-class restraint which makes the flowering of genius impossible. From his infancy onwards he had kept Wolfgang in a moral strait-jacket; it never struck him that it might have been as uncomfortable as a suit of mail. Whilst enduring all the strain of composing immortal works and giving brilliant concert performances, the boy was expected to conform to the daily restrictions of an ordered, subservient life. The wonder is that Wolfgang was

until his twenty-fifth year so pliable, so affectionate, so devoted
to his father, that the strain never became a conscious burden
to him until then. But with maturity came the resolve to throw
off at last both the Archbishop's throttling yoke and the
paternal harness.

That he was also a little dazzled by the glorious opportunities
Vienna seemed to be offering him in 1781 is undeniable. And
his optimism was at first justified. He was unquestionably the
greatest living composer and performer of keyboard concertos of
the time, and as such was in constant demand. He also had no
difficulty in finding pupils among the ladies of the aristocracy.

Frau Weber still had three unmarried daughters to provide
for—Josefa, Constanze, and Sophie. All of them did their
best to make their lodger as comfortable as possible. He rose
and dressed as he wished and if he were busy composing in
the evenings, dinner would be postponed to suit his convenience,
often until ten o'clock.

Unfortunately, however, complications soon arose, even in
this congenial environment. The Weber's lodger was a normal,
healthy young man, surrounded by three girls who must
inevitably have set their caps at him, even though he had
been in love not so long ago with their now successfully married
sister. Josefa was already too old for him, Sophie too young.
Constanze, eighteen, was just the right age.

Both before and after their marriage Wolfgang always
insisted on the fact that she was not pretty, although she had
large expressive dark eyes and a neat figure and also sang
quite nicely. But an attractive girl, with what is nowadays
known as sex appeal, could nevertheless be a dangerous
house-mate for a young man of his age and temperament.
And people were beginning to comment, for the Viennese
were always notorious for love of gossip and scandal-mongering.
Needless to say Leopold had his spies in Vienna; Constanze now
appeared to him just as dangerous a seductress as Aloysia
had seemed a few years ago.

At the end of July Wolfgang found himself compelled to
seek another lodging, much against his will:

Vienne, ce 25 de juillet, 1781

. . . I am very sorry that I am obliged to do this on account
of silly talk, in which there is not a word of truth. I should very

much like to know what pleasure certain people can find in spreading entirely groundless reports. Because I am living with them, therefore I am going to marry the daughter. There has been no talk of our being in love. They have skipped that stage. No, I just take rooms in the house and *marry*. If ever there was a time when I thought less of getting married, it is most certainly now! For (although the last thing I want is a rich wife) even if I could now make my fortune by a marriage, I could not possibly pay court to anyone, for my mind is running on very different matters.

And that was the truth. For five days later he wrote in triumph to inform Leopold that Stephanie had kept his promise to give him a German opera to compose. The title was *Belmonte und Konstanze*, or *Die Verführung aus dem Serail*, later to be known as *Die Entführung* and in English as *The Abduction from the Seraglio*, or, in short, *The Seraglio*.

It has often been suggested that Mozart called the heroine of this enchantingly gay work Constanze in honour of Miss Weber. But the similarity in their names was merely a coincidence. The story of *Belmonte und Konstanze* had been written originally in 1780, and produced as an opera in Berlin with music by another composer, Johann André. Stephanie simply proposed to produce another version of it, with music by Mozart.

Wolfgang continued his letter to Leopold, quoted above, with the bald statement that he was not in love with Miss Weber although 'I fool about and have fun with her when time permits (which is only in the evenings when I take supper at home, for in the morning I write in my room and in the afternoon I am rarely in the house) and—that is all.' Nevertheless, he was obliged, most reluctantly, to move from his comfortable rooms in the Auge Gottes. At the end of August he had found another lodging, which, even had he not contrasted it unfavourably with his previous one, was impossible:

Vienne, ce 22 d'Aout, 1781

The owner's wife herself called the house a rats' nest . . . Ah, what a splendid dwelling for me, indeed, who have to receive visits from various distinguished people.

Shortly afterwards he found a better abode, but even so 'I swear to you that if you had not wanted me to move into another lodging, I should not have left the Webers; for I feel just like a person who has left his own comfortable travelling carriage for a post-chaise.' Nagged by Leopold and harassed by these sordid problems, he was nevertheless working with tremendous enthusiasm at *The Seraglio*, the libretto of which he and Stephanie had altered to his liking, and which he found intensely stimulating.

The story tells how Constanze, a lovely young Spanish noblewoman, is captured by pirates, together with her English maid, Blonde, and Pedrillo, servant to Constanze's faithful lover, Belmonte. They are all three sold into slavery to the Turkish Pasha, Selim, in whose country palace by the shores of the Bosphorus the action passes. Pedrillo had got in touch with his handsome young master, the Spanish aristocrat, Belmonte, who arrives there to rescue them. Selim is honourably in love with Constanze, but she, true to Belmonte, refuses and defies her elderly possessor. The two couples attempt to escape, but are discovered and brought before the Pasha. Contrary to their sad expectation of torture and death, he pardons and releases them and they all happily sail away to home and freedom.

The part of the Pasha Selim was to be spoken only. Belmonte is a lyric tenor, Pedrillo a baritone and the bass part is that of Osmin, the Pasha's steward, an enormous, greedy, lecherous old man, and one of the greatest comic creations in all opera.

The Seraglio was the first great German comedy opera, or Singspiel. Mozart did not invent this form either; he took it over and both in *The Seraglio* and later in *The Magic Flute* lifted it to the highest musical plane. And whereas until then operatic parts had been merely vehicles for singers already engaged by the opera houses where the works were performed, in Osmin Mozart created the first real 'character' in opera— as much a 'character' as Falstaff or Mr Micawber. The part of Osmin is what in the theatre is known as 'cast-iron' or foolproof; when sung by a great singer it is irresistible and even a mediocre one can hardly altogether ruin it.

Fortunately, Mozart had been given a very good singer to interpret the role—Karl Ludwig Fischer—and was able to provide him with ample scope for his splendid low notes. His letters to his father, written as he was composing the work, reveal how marvellously he understood both human nature and the stage:

> 'As Osmin's rage gradually increases, there comes (just when the aria seems to be at an end) the *allegro assai*, which is in a totally different measure and in a different key; this is bound to be very effective. For just as a man in a towering rage oversteps all the bounds of order, moderation and propriety and completely forgets himself, so must the music too forget itself. But as passions, whether violent or not, must never be expressed in such a way as to excite disgust, and as music, even in the most terrible situations, must never offend the ear, but must please the hearer, or in other words must never cease to be *music*, I have gone from F (the key in which the aria is written), not into a remote key, but into a related one.'

The Seraglio is throughout conceived in a vein of comedy, with the exception of the great coloratura aria, 'Martern aller Arten', 'Torture me and flay me', in which Constanze defies the Pasha. This is really more like a concerto for the voice, similar to the concertos for the clavier Mozart was writing at the time. But when well sung it is also highly dramatic and effective.

The Seraglio was not produced until July 1782. In the meantime a dramatic change had also taken place in the life of its composer.

3

The first hint of this impending change, in Mozart's correspondence during the autumn of 1781, occurs in a letter to his Bäserl in Augsburg. The difference between its tone and content and those of his earlier flippant, naughty communications, is striking. It was written with two distinct motives. The first was to make clear to her, in the most tactful, gentle manner possible, that if she had ever entertained ideas of marriage with him, these must now finally be set aside. The second was to inform her, with his usual frankness, 'that the gossip which people have been so kind as to circulate about me, is partly true and partly false'. That gossip concerned his relations with Constanze Weber. One of his greatest anxieties at the time was how to break the news, or rather the facts, to his father. His letters to Leopold were now composed almost as carefully as musical works. He first alluded to the situation *piano, piano,* in veiled terms, at the end of a long and maliciously amusing account of a Court Ball at the Palace of Schönbrunn. But in the last paragraph there was a change of tone to deep seriousness: 'You say that I must remember that I have an immortal soul. Not only do I think it, but I firmly believe it. If it were not so, wherein would consist the difference between men and beasts? Just because I both know and most firmly believe this, I have not been able to carry out all your wishes exactly in the way you expected.' This, of course, brought an immediate reaction from Leopold. Wolfgang's next letter was in the same vein. He presented his father with the statement, as carefully phrased as possible, but leaving no further room for doubt whatever, that he was engaged to be married to Constanze. But before doing so, he led up to this information by a long account and explanation of his sex-life hitherto, an admirably simple and candid plea for understanding that is surely one of the most moving ever written by a loving son to an autocratic old father from whose despotism he has at last freed himself:

> Vienne, ce 15 de Decbre, 1781
> . . . I am very anxious to secure here a small but *certain* income which . . . will enable me to live here quite comfortably —and then—to marry! You are horrified at the idea? But I entreat you, dearest, most beloved father, to listen to me . . . The voice of nature speaks as loud in me as in others . . . I simply cannot live as most young men do in these days. In the first place, I have too much religion; in the second place, I have too great a love of my neighbour and too high a feeling of honour to seduce an innocent girl; and, in the third place, I have too much horror and disgust, too much dread and fear of diseases and too much care for my health to fool about with whores. So I can swear that I have never had relations of that sort with any woman . . . I stake my life on the truth of what I have told you.

He next explained that 'I who from my youth up have never been accustomed to look after my own belongings, linen, clothes, and so forth, cannot think of anything more necessary to me than a wife', and clinched the argument by pointing out —and what young man in similar circumstances has failed to do so?—that two can live as cheaply as one, or certainly no more expensively.

He then confessed who was the object of his love, imploring Leopold not to be 'horrified again': 'Surely not one of the Webers? Yes, one of the Webers . . . Constanze, the middle one . . . the martyr of the family . . . She is not ugly, but at the same time far from beautiful. Her whole beauty consists in two little black eyes and a pretty figure . . . I love her and she loves me with all her heart . . . when I resigned the Archbishop's service, our love had not yet begun. It was born of her tender care and attention when I was living in their house.'

During the nineteenth century and even until the present day, there has been a great deal of controversy about Mozart's marriage. And in discussing it the greatest caution is necessary, for although the facts are well known they have been interpreted in more than one way by some of his biographers, to suit their own emotional reactions to the situation. Did Constanze, as Wolfgang claimed in his letters to Leopold, truly love him, or was she, as has been alleged, a designing minx in league with her mother to entrap the poor innocent young man into matrimony?

Mozart was more capable than many young men in love of telling the truth, even when it was to his own disadvantage. His account to his father of his sexual life (or rather lack of it) until 1781, rings impeccably true. The truth and nothing but the truth, yes. But was it also, at that time, the whole truth? No. For more details emerged in a later letter, on 22 December. A certain Herr von Winter, a Mannheim violinist and composer, had given Leopold a version of what had been happening in Vienna which infuriated Wolfgang, and which he described as a pack of lies. But it was necessary for him to refute them as best he could by sending his father his own version: 'Well, let's come to the marriage contract, or rather to the written assurance of my honourable intentions towards the girl . . . as the father is no longer alive a guardian has taken his place.' This guardian was Herr Johann von Thorwart, an administrator of the Viennese National Theatre. 'The mother knows me and knows that I am honourable . . . but the guardian told the mother to forbid me to associate with her daughter until I had come to a written agreement with him . . . What other course was open to me? I had either to give him a written contract or—to desert the girl. What man who loves sincerely and honestly can forsake his beloved? . . . So I drew up a document to the effect *that I bound myself to marry Mlle Constanze Weber within the space of three years and that if it should prove impossible for me to do so owing to my changing my mind, she should be entitled to claim from me three hundred gulden a year* . . . But what did the angelic girl do when the guardian was gone? She asked her mother for the document, and said to me: "*Dear Mozart! I need no written assurance from you. I believe what you say*," and tore up the paper.'

Wolfgang had asked von Thorwart to give him his word of honour that he would keep the matter to himself until Mozart had obtained his father's consent to the marriage. But the story was soon all over Vienna and so reached Leopold's ears. Needless to say, he took the worst possible view of this alleged plot. In his opinion Herr von Thorwart and Madame Weber 'should be put in chains, made to sweep streets and have boards hung round their necks with the words "*seducers of youth*" '.

On 16 January 1782, Wolfgang wrote, quoting these words with the smilingly adult comment 'That too is an exaggeration.' He admitted that Madame Weber and Constanze's guardian had evidently acted somewhat hastily, but was clearly un-influenced either by them or by his father's wrath. He dismissed the matter in four words—'But enough of this', continuing his letter with an account of a pianistic duel between himself and his rival, the fashionable pianist and composer, Muzio Clementi, which had taken place at the invitation of the Emperor.

In his biography of Mozart, Alfred Einstein sided with Leopold's view, and went even further. He described that tiresome, tippling old future mother-in-law of his, Frau Weber, as Mozart's Queen of the Night, an evil, positively sinister influence in his life. Constanze was alleged to be no better than she should have been, heartless and mercenary. But, even disregarding Wolfgang's conviction that she was nothing of the kind and an honourable, angelic girl, the behaviour of her mother and guardian could have been completely justified on social and moral grounds with no sinister intention whatever. She was not yet twenty, poor, but honest. Her talents and looks were not such as would easily procure a dowerless girl a husband, had she not been fortunate enough to have appealed to young Mozart as a suitable bride. He had lived in the house for some time, he had, on his own admission, 'fooled around' with her. Whilst, according to him, her mother did trust him, there had been sufficient gossip to compel him, most unwillingly, to seek other, far less congenial and comfortable lodgings. Supposing that the 'fooling' had gone just too far, there was no doubt at all that in that case Constanze would have been, in the parlance of the period, 'ruined'. Her prospects of any other marriage would have been nil; matters had already gone sufficiently far for her name to have been compromised. In the circumstances, almost any prudent father or guardian would have insisted as hers did, on the young man giving some guarantee of his intentions and of making some small provision for the girl if he let her down. Mozart wrote to his father that he had signed the contract with the greatest willingness, 'for I knew that I should never have to pay these three hundred gulden, because I shall never forsake her'.

When Constanze impulsively tore up her fiancé's written promise of marriage she behaved exactly as any girl in love, at any period, would have done. But according to Einstein, 'with this noble gesture Constanze only enmeshed the fly more securely in the web'. He adds, naïvely, 'Mozart's . . . inability to break out of the web that was spun around him is very hard to understand. For Mozart could be very rough in dealing with women who had designs upon him.' And in fact he was rough with old Frau Weber, refusing firmly to set up house with her when he and Constanze were married.

There seems to have been little enough mystery about the whole business, or need for more pressure on the part of Constanze's mother and guardian than necessary to see that the girl was made an honest woman of. For when Wolfgang wrote to his father that he wanted and needed both a wife and housewife he was writing the simple truth. Had there been in Vienna at the time a crowd of eligible young ladies eager and willing to marry a small, temperamental, probably gifted but still only moderately successful young composer with doubtful prospects (and whose fathers or guardians would have been prepared to give their consent to such a match) Wolfgang might have had second thoughts with regard to Constanze

Weber. But at that time she was the only one prepared to take the risk.

We know that the Webers were in many ways unconventional and even 'bohemian' and these very easy-going characteristics made them congenial to Wolfgang, who had been brought up in a strictly conventional manner but was nevertheless no saint or ascetic. He himself thoroughly enjoyed flirtation and sexual banter, even although he had so carefully drawn the line between them and anything in the nature of libertinage and was almost certainly a virgin until his marriage. At the end of April 1782, his courtship of Constanze appears to have included a lovers' quarrel, provoked by slightly unseemly conduct on her part. She had told her sisters—in his presence—that she had permitted a young dandy (known in the Viennese French of the period as a '*chapeau*') to tie a ribbon around her calves to measure their width. There is no evidence except Wolfgang's letter to her of 29 April, 1782, to prove that any such incident had in fact occurred. He had reiterated so often to other people his opinion that she was not pretty that he had probably expressed it equally openly to her face. It would have been only too natural had Constanze retaliated by thinking up this little plot in order to arouse his jealousy, and whether this was the case or not he certainly reacted very strongly. They quarrelled: 'In spite of all my entreaties you have thrown me over three times and told me to my face that you intend to have nothing more to do with me.' He continued his letter by giving her a lecture on behaviour seemly in a young woman betrothed to be married, and it would not be at all surprising had Constanze, on reading it, broken into delighted girlish giggles at the success of her little plot.

There had been further rows and quarrels in the Weber household after Constanze had torn up the marriage contract. Wolfgang had no doubt told the story of his love troubles to his friend and patroness, the Baroness von Waldstädten. This lady had offered to take Constanze into her home, and it was there that the alleged incident with the '*chapeau*' had taken place. The jealous lover continued his letter: 'If it be true that the Baroness herself allowed it to be done to her, the case is still quite different, for she is already past her prime and cannot possibly attract any longer—and besides she is inclined to be promiscuous with her favours.'

By 8 May the lovers had made it up again. Constanze was also making up dresses for her trousseau. Both she and Wolfgang were attempting to ingratiate themselves with Leopold and Nannerl in Salzburg. Nannerl had always taken a great interest in fashion and Wolfgang's letters now alluded to this, containing messages on Constanze's behalf with regard to the latest Viennese modes. Nannerl, in spite of such presents— dresses, ribbons, frills and fripperies—nevertheless did not respond with equal ardour to such messages as the postscript to Wolfgang's letter to his father on 29 May:

> P.S.—My dear Constanze kisses your hands and embraces my sister as her true friend and future sister-in-law.

The Seraglio was produced on 16 July 1782. Unfortunately Mozart had already made certain bitter enemies and on the first and second nights there was a great deal of organized opposition: 'Yesterday there was an even stronger cabal against it than on the first evening! The whole first act was accompanied by hissing. But indeed they could not prevent the loud shouts of "bravo" during the arias', and, even more important to a young man impatient to marry: 'My opera has brought in 1,200 gulden in the two days.'

Wolfgang was continuing to urge his father to give his permission to his marriage when at the beginning of August his hand was abruptly forced. Constanze was still living with Baroness von Waldstädten. He wrote to the Baroness, clearly in considerable alarm: 'Madame Weber's maid-servant has brought me my music, for which I have had to give her a written receipt. She has also told me something in confidence which, although I do not believe it could happen, as it would be a disgrace to the whole family, yet seems possible when one remembers Madame Weber's stupidity, and which consequently causes me anxiety. It appears that Sophie—(Constanze's younger sister)—went to the maid-servant in tears and when the latter asked her what was the matter, she said: "Do tell Mozart in secret to arrange for Constanze to go home, for my mother is absolutely determined to have her fetched by the police." Are the police in Vienna allowed to go into any house? Perhaps the whole thing is only a trap to make her return home. But if it could be done, then the best plan I can think of is to marry Constanze to-morrow morning,—or even to-day, if that is possible. For I should not like to expose my beloved one to this scandal—and there could not be one if she were my wife.'

There seems little evidence, except for the servant's gossip, that Frau Weber seriously intended to have the police fetch her daughter home, although she quite probably uttered the threat in a moment of bad temper. Being nagged by Herr von Thorwart and suspecting that even if Wolfgang's intentions really were honourable Leopold Mozart would withhold his consent to the marriage as long as possible, she no doubt found that the situation was getting on her nerves to an intolerable degree. Moreover, Frau Weber's anger with her daughter abated as soon as Wolfgang and Constanze were married at last—on 4 August 1872. She, Sophie, and Herr von Thorwart attended the wedding, the guardian as witness both for the bride and groom. The Baroness gave a supper-party for them which Wolfgang described to Leopold as 'indeed more princely than baronial'. His father could no longer withhold his consent to the *fait accompli*, although he gave himself the petty satisfaction of writing to inform the Baroness that his son could expect no further financial support from him.

A fortnight later Wolfgang signed a letter to Leopold with his own name, W. A. Mozart, under which he wrote:

> Man and wife
> Are one life

and several of his later letters were signed 'your most obedient children W: et C: Mozart'. It does not appear that he did so in any sense defiantly, but merely in the first flush of pride of a newly-wed young husband. Nevertheless, Wolfgang's marriage did in fact mark his final emancipation from his long submission to paternal authority.

PART THREE: MANHOOD

Chapter VIII

MARRIAGE

IN what kind of world and in what setting did Mozart spend the adult years of his life, those in which he was to produce his greatest musical creations at almost breathless speed?

It was a world of flux, of transition from one historical period to another. The last twenty years of the eighteenth century were to be as important to us as to those who lived then, for their intellectual, political and social upheavals have not even now lost their impetus. This period witnessed the end of European serfdom and the outbreak of the French Revolution, which had the most profound influence on world history.

The Revolution of 1789 was not the mere creation of a few gifted intellectuals—scientists and philosophers, poets and dramatists. For their minds were stimulated by the mute yet powerful upsurge of the sense of fraternity and equality and the longing for liberty of the common man. Millions of peasants were in revolt against the chains of feudalism which bound them still to the service of their overlords and masters, who, in their turn, were desperately endeavouring to stem this rising tide and to preserve their ancient rights. The Catholic Church, too, was fighting to retain its power over men's minds and souls in face of the advancing revolutionary atheism or idealistic monotheism that were astir, either in political movements like Jacobinism, or semi-religious, like Freemasonry.

On her death in 1780 Maria Theresa had reigned over the Austro-Hungarian Empire for forty years. After the death of her husband, the Emperor Francis I, in 1765, her son Joseph reigned jointly with his mother. Joseph II was one of the most interesting and in some ways sympathetic of absolute monarchs. He aspired to be a benevolent despot—a contradiction in terms, since politically despotism and benevolence are almost impossible bedfellows. Joseph himself was conscientious and generous, filled with a vague sentimental goodwill towards his people and influenced intellectually by his fellow-ruler and rival, Frederick the Great of Prussia. But the co-regency was marked, naturally, by constant rows between the imperial mother—who thought that an Empire, like a family, should be governed by 'gentle violence'—and her son, who was determined to free his peasant subjects from the great feudal landowners whom he regarded as their oppressors.

When Maria Theresa died Joseph became sole Emperor and, free of the maternal yoke, proceeded to put his reforms into practice with more enthusiasm than discrimination. Like his mother, he had a very high sense of duty and moral responsibility. Like her, he equated 'the Good' with his own person— for he was not only the ruler of Austria but the Holy Roman Emperor—and 'Evil' with the plans and aspirations of those lesser men who strove to thwart his divine mission.

The result was that although no monarch ever paved his road to hell with better intentions, owing to the intellectual confusion which beset him he trusted no one and alienated his ministers and counsellors. He was to know the full bitterness of failure and frustration when shortly before his death in 1790 he was obliged to retract all the reforms he had spent his reign in introducing.

In appearance Joseph was elegant, almost handsome; in manner charming and affable. Unlike so many monarchs of his day he had been extremely happily married, to Princess Isabella of Parma. It was his greatest personal tragedy that she died in 1763, childless. His second marriage in 1767 was a political alliance with Princess Josepha of Bavaria; it was as miserable a failure as his first had been a success. He had no children by her, either, and was succeeded on his own death by his brother, Leopold II.

Joseph of course found amorous distractions. His most intimate women friends included the Countess Thun, one of Mozart's earliest Viennese patronesses. During the 1780's, his Court was the second most fashionable and certainly the gayest in all Europe. He was extremely musical as well as pleasure-loving, a great patron of musicians and especially of Italian opera. The most famous opera composer and librettist of the day—Gluck and Metastasio—had for long made their homes in Vienna. As in Paris and London Italian opera was the delight of the aristocracy and the world of fashion. Vienna was crowded with Italian composers, chief among them a protégé of Gluck's, Antonio Salieri, on whose works the Emperor doted.

Joseph II housed the entire Italian opera company in his palace, where they lived, dined and wined most generously at his expense. He took a personal interest in their lives and careers. He himself ate and drank moderately but had a passion for chocolate drops, which he carried in his waistcoat pocket and would be constantly popping into his mouth.

At the very beginning of Wolfgang's career as a prodigy Leopold had complained to Hagenauer of the bitter antagonism of the Italian musicians at the Court of the Elector of Bavaria. Their enmity pursued Mozart, even as a child, both in Paris and London, and on his second visit to Paris in 1778 the Italians were so firmly entrenched in favour there that he was unable to obtain an opera commission.

This vendetta culminated in Vienna, where the Italian composers, chief among them Salieri, tried from the outset to poison the atmosphere against him by spreading the most outrageous lies and slanders, which even reached the Emperor's notice.[1]

While it is true that Salieri and his friends would cheerfully have cut Mozart's throat or poisoned him—and the legend was long believed that Salieri had actually attempted the latter—he did not make life easier for himself either.

Even when he was still in the Archbishop's service Mozart had been hoping and angling for some Court appointment. He had been a minor favourite of Joseph II's ever since his early appearances at his mother's Court as an infant prodigy. In December 1781, Wolfgang proudly wrote to Leopold that 'At table the other day the Emperor gave me the very highest praise, accompanied by the words: *"C'est un talent décidé!"* ' In

---

[1] Edward Holmes, Mozart's first English biographer, described the situation very well in his *Life*, published in 1845 (p. 148): 'Musical history can scarcely parallel the animosity, the jealousy and spirit of base intrigue which prevailed at this time among the composers of Vienna, of whom each was the guardian of his own little interests at the expense of everything else in life. To the numerous intrigues and repeated slanders of which Mozart was the subject, he had nothing to oppose but his rectitude of principle and transcendent genius; yet as the latter, during his lifetime, through malicious arguments and ignorant judgment, was sometimes brought into question, his enemies not unfrequently gained their point by adding to the difficulties of his existence.'

Constanze Mozart. Portrait by Josef Lange (1782)

[face p. 86

Mozart. Silverpoint drawing by Dora Stock, 1789

the following April he informed Leopold that: 'I have said nothing to you about the rumour you mention of my being certainly taken into the Emperor's service, because I myself know nothing about it. It is true that here too the whole town is ringing with it and that a number of people have already congratulated me . . . But up to this moment I have no definite information.' And nothing did come of this rumour, in spite of all the efforts of its subject and his friends at Court. One of the most important of these was the diplomat, Baron van Swieten, to whose house 'I go every Sunday at twelve o'clock, where nothing is played but Handel and Bach'. This study of the works of the Bach family, and especially the fugues of Johann Sebastian, was to have a profound influence on Mozart's own later musical style.

But the allegation that he was insufferably conceited was not without some foundation in truth. After his marriage to Constanze, when even he himself realized that his prospects of a Court appointment were not yet about to mature, Wolfgang wrote to his father: 'There is no monarch in the world whom I should be more glad to serve than the Emperor, but I refuse to beg for any post. I believe that I am capable of doing credit to any Court. If Germany, my beloved fatherland . . . will not accept me, then in God's name let France or England become the richer by another talented German, to the disgrace of the German nation,' a statement that, although perfectly true, was yet made with the rash arrogance of disappointed youth. His intention to try his luck once again in France or England was abandoned on Leopold's advice.

In spite of his desire to be employed by him, Wolfgang was not above contradicting his royal patron himself when it came to musical matters. On one occasion His Majesty had banteringly criticized an aria he had written: 'Too many notes, my dear Mozart, too many notes.' To which the young composer respectfully no doubt but firmly replied: 'Just as many notes, Sire, as necessary, and no more.'

He was a bit of a fop, too, fond as are many small men of fine clothes, lace and jewellery. Muzio Clementi, his rival performer on the piano, maliciously stated that when on one occasion Mozart appeared at Court he was so bewigged and bedecked that he was mistaken for a flunkey!

2

During the first years of his married life, however, Mozart was doing very nicely. Even his enemies could not assail his reputation as the most brilliant composer and performer of piano concertos of his time and as such he was constantly employed, giving concert after concert, both in private houses and in public, attended by the aristocracy with both social and financial success. During those years he also continued to produce a prodigious amount of vocal and instrumental music.

Wolfgang was well aware of the fact that his father and sister were still unreconciled to his marriage. He hoped, however, that when they met his 'little wife' they would take her to their hearts. After he had given up his intention of visiting France and England he was most anxious to bring Constanze to Salzburg to stay with them. The visit, planned for the winter of 1782, had to be postponed until the following summer, for Constanze was pregnant. She gave birth to their first child, a boy, on 17 June 1783. In his letter to Leopold on the following day, Wolfgang informed him that the child had been christened Raimund Leopold—the former being the name of his friend and patron Baron Wetzlar, who stood godfather to the baby. This letter contains the information that 'the child has been given to a foster-nurse against my will, or rather at my wish! For I was quite determined that whether she should be able to do so or not, my wife was never to feed her child. Yet I was equally determined that my child was never to take the milk of a stranger! I wanted the child to be brought up on water, like my sister and myself. However, the midwife, my mother-in-law, and most people here have begged and implored me not to allow it, if only for the reason that most children here who are brought up on water do not survive, as the people here don't know how to do it properly. That induced me to give in, for I should not like to have anything to reproach myself with.'

In the eighteenth century it was the practice in the higher ranks of society to board out new-born infants with their wet-nurses. So it was not unusual that Wolfgang and Constanze should have left the baby in Vienna when they departed for Salzburg at the beginning of August. The unfortunate infant died on the 19th of that month. It is useless to speculate on whether he might or might not have survived had his father been allowed to rear him on water instead of milk.

Wolfgang had made a vow that if he and Constanze were married he would write a Mass for her, which should be sung in Salzburg. He had composed most of it but it was still apparently unfinished when they went there, having no doubt been left uncompleted owing to the pressure of more urgent work at that time. However, the necessary parts were added to it from one of his earlier Masses, and his vow was fulfilled when it was performed in Salzburg on 25 August 1783. Constanze, who had quite a pretty voice, herself sang the soprano part. She also made every effort to ingratiate herself with her in-laws. But neither Leopold nor Marianne could overcome their prejudice against her, which was probably no stronger than Wolfgang's own dislike of his birthplace. It must have been a relief to the whole family when the young couple returned home. Wolfgang continued to write most affectionately, however, both to his father and sister, and Constanze to send little presents to her sister-in-law.

In 1784 Nannerl at last got married. She was by then 34, a not particularly good-looking spinster. Her bridegroom, Baron Berchtold zu Sonnenburg, was a widower in his early fifties, with five children by his former marriage. They lived in St Gilgen, where Frau Mozart had been born. Wolfgang wrote to congratulate his sister on her marriage, enclosing a charming little poem, but neither he nor his wife attended the wedding.

In the following September Constanze bore her second son, Karl Thomas, who, luckier than his elder brother, lived until 1858.

After Nannerl's marriage Wolfgang worried a good deal about Leopold, who was now living all alone in Salzburg. So in February 1785, he persuaded his father to visit him in Vienna, where Leopold stayed with his son until the end of April.

Constanze has been accused of having been a very bad and extravagant housekeeper. Yet in the letters Leopold wrote from Vienna to his daughter he never criticized his daughter-in-law on this score, which he almost certainly would have done had he found her an incompetent or negligent housewife: 'That your brother has very fine quarters with all the necessary furniture you may gather from the fact that his rent is 460 gulden.' And: 'If my son *has no debts to pay*, I think that he can now lodge two thousand gulden in the bank. Certainly the money is there and so far as eating and drinking is concerned, the housekeeping is extremely economical.'

But Wolfgang always had debts to pay. From the time of his marriage until his death he never ceased to be in financial difficulties. The basic reason for this was, as he himself constantly asserted, the fact that he had no regular appointment which would bring him in a steady income, apart from his irregular earnings as composer, performer, and teacher. At the time of Leopold's visit he was at the height of his Viennese success and was giving recitals and concerts almost every evening. Leopold was growing old and the pace was rather too hot for his comfort: 'As usual it will probably be one o'clock before we get to bed. Every day there are concerts and the whole time is given up to teaching, music, composing and so forth. I feel rather out of it all. If only the concerts were over! It is impossible for me to describe the rush and bustle!' But the highlight of Leopold's stay in Vienna was the visit to Mozart of his elder colleague and devoted friend, Joseph Haydn.

It is delightful to contemplate—even at a distance of nearly two hundred years—the mutual admiration and affection for one another of Mozart and Haydn. His younger brother, Michael Haydn, was also a gifted composer, especially of Masses, but either because of his marital troubles—his wife was a shrew—or because of professional disappointments, he was over-fond of the bottle. Leopold, ever censorious and priggish, could not abide drunkards, all the more if they were living and working in such close proximity to himself. He often referred disapprovingly to Michael Haydn's habits, but with his usual integrity never on that account withheld his admiration for his talents. On one occasion, when Michael Haydn was either too unwell or unsober to write two violin and viola duets which the Archbishop had commanded from him, Wolfgang (who himself loved a glass of good wine) came to his rescue by composing them instead.

Joseph ('Papa') Hadyn was one of the sweetest-natured men who ever lived. Although he was old enough to be Mozart's father he was one of the first to recognize his genius and remained all his life his steadfast champion. And Wolfgang had realized at a very early stage that Joseph Haydn had found the true idiom of German chamber music, especially of string quartets. Inspired by these he himself composed a set of six similar quartets between 1782 and 1785, which he dedicated to Haydn in a charmingly turned letter in Italian, referring to these works as his 'six sons' and entrusting them 'to the protection of a man who was very celebrated at the time and who, moreover, happened to be his best friend'.

A day or two after his arrival in Vienna Leopold wrote to Nannerl: 'On Saturday evening Herr Joseph Haydn and the two Barons Tinti came to see us and the new quartets were performed . . . Haydn said to me: "Before God and as an honest man I tell you that your son is the greatest composer known to me either in person or by name. He has taste and what is more, the most profound knowledge of composition." '

When Haydn was fifty-eight he was invited to London, where he had an enormous success. He had been most anxious to take Wolfgang there but the plan did not mature. In 1790 Mozart took him to an instrumental rehearsal of his opera *Così Fan Tutte*, one of the last occasions when they met. Soon afterwards they parted in tears, never to meet again. For Mozart died in 1791, whilst Haydn was in London. Even their great devotion to one another did not escape the smears and calumnies of their Italian enemies and detractors, but fortunately these had no success. Haydn was too generous and too serious in his musical judgement to be influenced by such malice; Mozart, too devoted to Haydn and to his music.

Chapter IX

'NOTHING BUT "FIGARO" . . .'

IN 1786 Mozart was thirty years old and had still not received any regular appointment. Although he was working night and day at composition, teaching, and performance, his financial difficulties always seemed to outstrip his earnings. In the previous November he had had to turn for temporary help to a music publisher, Franz Anton Hoffmeister. He had, however, had one small operatic success. For he had been given a commission to write a short one-act opera called *Der Schauspieldirektor* to a libretto by Stephanie, which was put on at Schönbrunn Palace and afterwards at the Kärntnertor Theatre. It was a trifle, but a charmingly gay one.

His great opportunity followed—as Leopold, who had by then returned to Salzburg, wrote to his sister on 11 November 1785: 'At last I have received a letter of twelve lines from your brother, dated November 2nd. He begs to be forgiven, as he is up to the eyes in work at his opera "Le Nozze di Figaro" . . . I know the piece; it is a very tiresome play and the translation from the French will certainly have to be altered very freely if it is to be effective as an opera. God grant that the text may be a success. I have no doubt about the music.' Once again, Leopold's irritation with his dilatory son was rectified by his unswerving confidence in his genius.

The 'tiresome' play in question was Caron de Beaumarchais's great satirical comedy, *Le Mariage de Figaro*. In spite of the opposition of Louis XVI it had been produced in Paris—at a private performance—on 27 April 1784. Joseph II followed his brother-in-law's prohibition and forbade the play to be performed in Vienna also. But when French public opinion compelled the King of France to withdraw his ban on it, the whole of European society was clamouring to see it.

Mozart's librettist was the Abbé da Ponte, a very colourful eighteenth-century character, a Venetian Jew who had become a Catholic priest and who had made a great reputation as a writer and adapter of comedies. He was a favourite of Joseph II's, whom he now persuaded to allow him to make an Italian adaptation of *Figaro* in operatic form.

It can easily be imagined what a powerful appeal the subject of the conflict between the valet and intellectual, Figaro, and the Spanish Count Almaviva, his reactionary and proud master, made to Mozart, who himself had been so long in servitude to a great overlord, subject to so many indignities, compelled to sit at table with Colloredo's valets. Moreover, even Figaro was not dismissed with a kick on the behind. Da Ponte cut out all the long speeches and monologues, which even had they not been so bitingly revolutionary would not have been suitable for musical treatment. But in the very first scene of the opera the conflict between master and servant is clearly brought out.

Figaro is to wed the charming Susanna, maid to the Countess. He is measuring up the bedroom between the apartments of their employers, in which, after their marriage, they are to sleep, 'the most convenient room in the castle'. But Susanna immediately enlightens him on the Count's motive in allocating it to them:

> Sus.: The plain fact is, my dear, that his lordship is tired of running after all the pretty girls of the neighbourhood, and means to try his luck at home—not with his own wife, but with yours . . . So you thought the dowry which my lord is giving me was the reward of *your* faithful service? . . . You're wrong. The dowry is to pay for a certain privilege belonging to the Lord of the Manor . . .

The privilege in question was the *jus primae noctis*, the right of a feudal overlord to deflower the bride of one of his serfs on her wedding night.

> Fig.: That abominable privilege! But he abolished it of his own free will, or I would never have married you within his dominions.
>
> Sus.: He abolished it, I know, but he means to buy it back on the sly.

Figaro then declares war on his perfidious employer in his cavatina ending with the threat:

> Try to deceive me, I'll do the same thing;
> Two play at that game, yes, Sir, believe me;
> I'll put a spoke in your wheel if I can.

which, with the Countess's and Susanna's help he does when, in the last act the Count, having made an assignation in the garden with Susanna, and the two women having changed into each other's dresses, is discovered making love to his own wife, whom he had intended to deceive as well as Figaro. The plot is complicated by the devotion to the Countess of a young page, Cherubino, whom the unfaithful but jealous Almaviva forthwith 'conscripts' into his own regiment. This situation leads to Figaro's most famous aria, 'Non piu andrai', one of the greatest Mozart ever wrote, and which immediately became the most popular tune of the day. Another complication is introduced in the character of the elderly Marcellina, who claims that Figaro has signed a contract to marry her, but who turns out to be his mother! The work is joyous throughout, packed with one lovely piece after another, solos and ensembles, disarmingly gay and lighthearted, and, in the Countess's exquisite solo, 'Dove sono' ('I remember days long departed, Days when love no end could know'), of touching lyrical beauty. Nevertheless the political satire was its mainspring as far as Mozart was concerned and shows through quite clearly. In our own time it is the most popular of all Mozart's operas and hardly a month goes by when it is not being performed in one country or another. The political implications have long ceased to have anything more than an historical interest; it survives purely as an operatic masterpiece.

But *Figaro* was only produced, originally, after endless struggles and difficulties. It had been commissioned to follow works by Gluck, Paisiello, and Salieri, as well as another Italian composer, Righini. The latter three were all vying with one another with cut-throat intrigues worthy of an Italian melodrama, but Mozart was, as usual, the chief target of his rivals. In April Leopold wrote to Nannerl: '*Le Nozze di Figaro* is being performed on the 28th for the first time. It will be surprising if it is a success, for I know that very powerful cabals have ranged themselves against your brother. Salieri and all his supporters will again try to move heaven and earth to down his opera.' It was first given on 1 May 1786, and in spite of Leopold's lugubrious forebodings was an instant success. But it was soon withdrawn from the Viennese repertoire and not revived there until much later.

The original Susanna was an Anglo-Italian singer, Nancy Storace, and the Basilio an Irish tenor, Michael Kelly, who adored Mozart and in his reminiscences left us the following delightful account of a rehearsal and of the production:

> All the original performers had the advantage of the instruction of the composer, who transfused into their minds his inspired meaning. I shall never forget his little animated countenance when lighted up with the glowing rays of genius: it is as impossible to describe as it would be to paint sunbeams . . .
>
> I remember at the first rehearsal of the full band, Mozart was on the stage with his crimson pelisse and gold-laced cocked hat, giving the time of the music to the orchestra. Figaro's song, 'Non piu andrai, farfallone amoroso', Bennuci gave with the greatest animation and power of voice. I was standing close to Mozart, who, *sotto voce*, was repeating, 'Bravo! Bravo! Bennuci'; and when Bennuci came to the final passage, 'Cherubino, alla vittoria, all gloria militar', which he gave out with stentorian lungs, the effect was electricity itself, for the whole of the performers on the stage, and those in the orchestra, as if actuated by one feeling of delight, vociferated 'Bravo! Bravo! Maestro! Viva, viva, grande Mozart'. Those in the orchestra I thought would never have ceased applauding, by beating the bows of their violins against the music-desks. The little man acknowledged, by repeated obeisances, his thanks for the distinguished mark of enthusiastic applause bestowed upon him.
>
> The same meed of approbation was given to the finale at the end of the first act; that piece of music alone, in my humble opinion, if he had never composed anything else as good, would have stamped him as the greatest master of his art . . . the *sestetto*, in the second act . . . was Mozart's favourite piece of the whole opera . . .
>
> At the end of the opera, I thought the audience would never have done applauding and calling for Mozart; almost every piece was encored, which prolonged it nearly to the length of two operas, and induced the Emperor to issue an order on the second representation that no piece of music should be encored. Never was anything more complete than the

triumph of Mozart, and his *Nozze di Figaro*, to which numerous overflowing audiences bore witness.

We are also indebted to Kelly for the following impressions of Mozart, that 'prodigy of genius' whom he first heard at a private concert where he 'favoured the company by performing fantasias and capriccios on the pianoforte. His feeling, the rapidity of his fingers, the great execution and strength of his left hand particularly, and the apparent inspirations of his modulations, astounded me'. Kelly, who had himself studied the piano as well as singing, was quite qualified to give this professional opinion.

> After this splendid performance we sat down to supper, and I had the pleasure to be placed at table between him and his wife, Madame Constance Weber, a German lady of whom he was passionately fond, and by whom he had three children. He conversed with me a good deal about Thomas Linley, the first Mrs Sheridan's brother, with whom he was intimate at Florence, and spoke of him with great affection. He said that Linley was a true genius, and he felt that, had he lived, he would have been one of the greatest ornaments of the musical world. After supper the young branches of our host had a dance, and Mozart joined them. Madame Mozart told me, that great as his genius was, he was an enthusiast at dancing . . .
>
> He was a remarkably small man, very thin and pale, with a profusion of fine fair hair, of which he was rather vain. He gave me a cordial invitation to his house, of which I availed myself, and passed a great deal of my time there. He always received me with kindness and hospitality. He was remarkably fond of punch, of which beverage I have seen him take copious draughts. He was also fond of billiards, and had an excellent billiard-table in his house. Many and many a game have I played with him, but always came off second-best. He gave Sunday concerts, at which I was never missing. He was kind-hearted and always ready to oblige, but so very particular, when he played, that if the slightest noise were made he instantly left off . . . Mozart was very liberal in giving praise to those who deserved it; but he felt a thorough contempt for insolent mediocrity.

Nancy Storace, who with Kelly had been engaged for the Vienna opera by the Austrian Ambassador in Italy, arrived there with her brother Stephen, who was to become one of late eighteenth-century England's most popular opera composers. They were the handsome and talented children of an Italian double-bass player in the Drury Lane orchestra; their mother, born in Bath, was also with them on this Continental trip. Nancy had an enormous success in Vienna. She and her brother, together with an English pupil of Mozart's, Thomas Attwood, who later became organist at St Paul's, were among his intimate friends. But it is highly unlikely that, as has been alleged, Wolfgang was ever seriously in love with Nancy Storace, or she with him. This gossip has only a slender foundation in the fact that just before the Storaces and Kelly, with Attwood, left Vienna to return to England, Mozart wrote an aria 'For Mademoiselle Storace and me', and himself played the piano accompaniment when she sang it. As these dear friends were leaving for London—and he himself would have been only too happy to have gone with them—he was naturally in a sentimental mood, and composed the recitative to the words, 'Ch'io mi scordi di te'—'How can I tear myself from thee?' Those of the aria, however, 'Do not fear, my beloved, that I will ever forget thee', were from *Idomeneo*. Moreover, as a letter from Leopold to Nannerl proves, Mozart was intending to take Constanze with him to England, which he would hardly have planned had he been following his beloved there.[1]

2

Neither Vienna nor Salzburg can rightfully claim the honour of having been the first city to recognize Mozart's genius. This must go to Prague, then the capital of Bohemia. *The Marriage*

[1] Nancy was still under eighteen when, in Vienna, she married an eccentric Englishman twenty years older than herself, a Dr John Fisher. The marriage was a very unhappy one; her husband ill-treated her so violently that she lost her voice for five months in consequence. Although the Emperor banished Fisher from Vienna in punishment, the husband may have had some grounds for his brutality. For sweet, pretty little Nancy was, in the language of the day, no better than she should have been. She became the mistress of one of the young 'bloods' then busily trying to paint the waters of the blue Danube red, Lord Barnard, later Duke of Cleveland. When the Storaces left Vienna he accompanied them. His affair with Nancy continued after they all arrived home, and to within three months of his marriage. Later, she lived with a famous tenor, John Braham, whose real name was Abraham, born in London of German-Jewish parents. She had a son by him. In due course, when she had become very stout and elderly, he left her. She dined with Michael Kelly on the night before her death. Although she bestowed her 'favours' freely, La Storace was more careful of her money than of her person, and is said to have left a fortune of £50,000.

of Figaro was produced there in December 1786—a mere eight months after its first performance in Vienna—and its success was riotous. The public was clamouring to pay homage to its composer and so in January Wolfgang and Constanze arrived in Prague, where they were the guests of Count Thun. The *Figaro* music was so much the rage that it was adapted for dancing. Mozart wrote to a friend in Vienna:

> Prague, January 14th, 1787
> . . . here they talk about nothing but 'Figaro'. Nothing is played, sung or whistled but 'Figaro'. No opera is drawing like 'Figaro'. Nothing, nothing but 'Figaro'. Certainly a great honour for me!

And as the result of this huge success, he was invited to compose another opera, especially for Prague. Da Ponte was again the librettist. But the subject was not so original a one as *Figaro*: it was, in fact, the very old one of Don Juan, or *Don Giovanni*.

Da Ponte, who was very busy with other work at the time simply 'lifted' and re-adapted the libretto from another Italian opera on this legendary theme. The cynical eighteenth century regarded the adventures of a libertine with a tolerant eye, especially if, as in Don Giovanni's case, they led him ultimately to hell.

In the first scene of Mozart's opera the Don kills the Commander, father of Donna Anna, whom he had been attempting to rape. The rest of the plot relates Anna's and her fiancé Ottavio's attempts to bring Don Giovanni to justice. Secondary themes are the pursuit of him by an ex-nun Elvira, whom he had seduced and then abandoned, but who still loves him desperately, and his amorous dalliance with a country lass, Zerlina. Following the well-known legend, Don Giovanni and his servant, Leporello, find themselves towards the end of the second act in the churchyard, in front of the assassinated Commander's statue. Jokingly, the Don invites his victim to supper. Gravely (if the pun may be excused) the statue nods its head in acceptance. And sure enough, it arrives. But there is nothing funny about its entrance. Don Giovanni is enjoying his succulent meal to the accompaniment of his private orchestra which plays, on stage, a selection from the most popular airs of the day, ending with 'Non piu andrai', when

Elvira comes to implore him once again to mend his ways. He merely laughs at her. Elvira goes and then rushes back, screaming with terror at the statue's approach. The Don sends Leporello after her and he, too, quakes with fear as the Commander, having ominously knocked on the door, is admitted by the imperturbable Don Giovanni. To the accompaniment of some of the most thrilling music Mozart ever wrote the statue drags the unrepentant seducer down to hell. The other characters then enter and point the moral in a light-hearted sextet.

As usual, Mozart had still been working on the score during rehearsals. On the eve of the opening performance, not one note of the overture had yet been written. Everyone was in a frenzy except the composer, for he knew that it only had to be written *down*. He sat up during the entire previous night doing so, whilst, as he tossed off sheet after sheet, Constanze loyally sat with him, keeping him awake with hot punch and light conversation. There was no time for a rehearsal next day of this thrilling overture, and the orchestra read it at sight at the first performance.

The work was conceived as a comic opera, although in the nineteenth century—especially in Germany—it was often produced as a tragic one. It contains one or two almost farcical scenes and lacks the intellectual satirical vein of *Figaro*. The characterization is also much less subtle. The autocratic, elegant Count Almaviva has been succeeded by the Don, a younger, more charming but also more frivolous nobleman. Figaro is replaced by his scoundrelly low-comedy servant Leporello, whom da Ponte modelled on a valet to his fellow-Venetian adventurer and friend, Casanova, the most celebrated seducer of the eighteenth century. Susanna, an intelligent and refined lady's maid, is replaced by Zerlina, a peasant girl, and a much more willing victim of a nobleman's amorous wiles. Rosina, the adorable Countess Almaviva, was a great lady with a sense of humour as well as a devoted wife. In *Don Giovanni* Anna, almost mad with grief at her father's murder, is otherwise a mere vehicle for a prima donna's vocalizations. Elvira is the only character in the work for whom one can feel some personal sympathy. The plot is clumsily put together; there are several long-winded and boring scenes.

Yet Mozart's genius set this dramatic hotch-potch to some

of the most glorious music ever written. What is more, all the music connected with the Commander—the natural and supernatural father whose murder gives the plot what little weight it has—is intensely dramatic, solemn, at moments even terrifying, and lifts the otherwise frivolous story on to an entirely different spiritual level.

Mozart had been commissioned to write this work in January 1787. After Leopold's visit to him and Constanze two years previously, he did not see his father again. During those two years he was most anxious to visit London and his English friends—the Storaces, Kelly, and his pupil Thomas Attwood— begged him to come with them when they returned home. It never occurred to him to leave Constanze behind. But they had two small children, Karl Thomas and another baby boy, who died when only a month old. Wolfgang had apparently requested his father to take these grandchildren into his care. This Leopold very definitely refused to do. 'You can easily imagine that I had to express myself very emphatically' (he wrote to Nannerl in November 1786) 'as your brother actually suggested that I should take care of his two children, because he was proposing to undertake a journey through Germany to England . . . Not at all a bad arrangement! They could go off and travel—they might even die—or remain in England—and I should have to run after them with the children. As for the payment which he offers me for the children and for maids to look after them, well—Basta! If he cares to do so, he will find my excuse very clear and instructive.'

At the beginning of the following spring the Storaces, Kelly, and Attwood all arrived in Salzburg. Leopold wrote to Nannerl on 1 March: 'As for your brother, I hear that he is back in Vienna. I had no reply to the letter I sent to him at Prague. The English company told me that he made a thousand gulden there, that little Leopold his last boy, had died, and that, as I had gathered, he wants to travel to England, but that his pupil is first going to procure a definite engagement for him in London . . . Probably Madame Storace and the whole company filled him with stories to the same effect and these people and his pupil must have first given him the idea of accompanying them to England. But no doubt after I sent him a fatherly letter, saying that he would gain nothing by a journey in summer, as he would arrive in England at the wrong time, that he ought to have at least two thousand gulden in his pocket before undertaking such an expedition, and finally that, unless he had procured in advance some definite engagement in London, he would have to be prepared, no matter how clever he was, to be hard up at first, at any rate, he has probably lost courage.' Wolfgang had returned to Vienna, and in his last letter to his father he made no further reference to any plan for visiting England.

Leopold was a good father according to his own lights and the tenets of his period, when parents were commonly stern and unrelenting towards their children, however gifted. His criticisms of the weaker sides of his son's character were often justified. He himself was respectable, self-righteous, and utterly unable to make allowances for the artistic temperament. Yet had it not been for Leopold's drive, organizing ability, and steadfast faith in Wolfgang's genius, Mozart might have spent his entire life in Salzburg, in the Archbishop's service, like his father. It was Leopold who showed him—and showed him to— the great world in which he belonged by divine right, who had taken him as a child to Paris and London. London was the place in which he had been happiest and to which he always longed to return. Yet now Leopold opposed this longing, unfortunately with success.

3

At the beginning of April Wolfgang learned that his father was seriously ill.

Vienna, April 4, 1787

. . . This very moment I have received a piece of news which greatly distresses me, the more so as I gathered from your last letter that, thank God, you were very well indeed. But now I hear that you are really ill. I need hardly tell you how greatly I am longing to receive some reassuring news from yourself. And I still expect it; although I have now made a habit of being prepared in all affairs of life for the worst. As death, when we come to consider it closely, is the true goal of our existence, I have formed during the last few years such close relations with this best and truest friend of mankind, that his image is not only no longer terrifying to me, but is indeed very soothing and consoling! And I thank my God for

> graciously granting me the opportunity (you know what I mean) of learning that death is the *key* which unlocks the door to our true happiness.

What was this opportunity, and why did Wolfgang so firmly assume that his father would know what he meant when he referred to it?

The answer is that this letter was written not only by a loving son to his sick father, but by a Freemason to a brother Mason.

Wolfgang had been initiated into the Masonic Order in 1784, and from that time onwards his spiritual and ethical standards were those of Freemasonry. Leopold had joined the Order when he had stayed with his son in Vienna a year later. Neither of them found these beliefs incompatible with Catholicism, in which they had been brought up, and from which they never seceded.

It is necessary to understand that whilst in the eighteenth century the Freemasons were intellectually on the side of the then revolutionary concepts of fraternity and equality—of universal brotherhood—they were not chiefly, as their enemies assumed, an atheistic or political organization. Maria Theresa's husband, the Emperor Francis I, had been a Freemason. But after his death, under pressure from her religious advisers, she had suppressed the Order and the Freemasons then went 'underground', in spite of the fact that many members of the Royal House and the aristocracy, as well as most of the leading intellectuals, joined them. To them there seemed no incompatibility between remaining members of the Church and belonging to their highly idealistic society, in spite of the fact that it had a series of rites and rituals regarded by the orthodox as wholly contrary to Catholicism. The Masonic concepts of life and death, brotherly love and divine benevolence, inspired Mozart with the deepest spiritual experiences of his manhood and with some of his greatest music, culminating in *The Magic Flute*. His allusions to death in this letter to Leopold find their explanation in the words of the High Priest Sarastro in that opera. When asked what would happen to the young Prince Tamino, if in the course of the tests he was to endure before being admitted to Sarastro's order he were to die, Sarastro replies: 'He will be

A street in Vienna during Mozart's lifetime—the Graben. (Carl Schütz, *c.* 1790)

Mozart at a performance of *Il Seraglio* at the Opera House in Berlin, 1789. From an engraving, possibly contemporary

in the hands of Osiris and Isis, and will know the joys of the
gods sooner than we ourselves.'

Wolfgang ended this letter to Leopold: 'I hope and trust that
whilst I am writing this you are feeling better. But if, contrary
to all expectations you are not recovering, I implore you by
. . . not to hide it from me, so that as quickly as is humanly
possible I may come to your arms. I entreat you by all that is
sacred—to both of us.' We do not, regrettably, know Leopold's
reply to this letter—if there was one. On 29 May Wolfgang
added a postscript to a note he had written to an intimate
friend, Baron Gottfried von Jacquin: 'I inform you that on
returning home today I received the sad news of my most
beloved father's death. You can imagine the state I am in.'

Leopold Mozart died on 28 May 1787. Wolfgang was then
a grown-up man, with a wife and son of his own. Yet in spite of
the successes he had won, he knew that he had not fulfilled his
father's hopes in him. Nor did he ever outgrow his father-
fixation and the feelings of guilt, whether repressed or not,
Leopold had inculcated into him since his adolescence. There
cannot be the slightest doubt of his genuine grief at Leopold's
death. But this may have been not altogether unmixed with
subconscious relief, which in its turn would have enhanced the
repressed guilt feelings. It would be surprising if these feelings
had not found some outlet in the grandiose and menacing
statue music in *Don Giovanni*.

Chapter X

PROUD POVERTY

WHEN Leopold died he was sixty-eight years old, a disappointed and embittered old man. In spite of Haydn's gratifying eulogies of Wolfgang's genius, his son had not fulfilled the great expectations his father had had of him. For Leopold, although loyal to the end to Wolfgang's superlative gifts, had expected him to make a bigger worldly success and to become, if not wealthy, at least prosperous. His disappointment is expressed in his very last letter, to Nannerl, written a fortnight before his death: 'Your brother is now living in the Landstrasse No. 224. He does not say why he has moved. Not a word. But unfortunately I can guess the reason.' The reason was, of course, that Wolfgang was as usual desperately hard up, and had again been compelled to move to a cheaper house.

The triumph of *Don Giovanni* in Prague was followed by what at first seemed another success. Wolfgang wrote to his sister at the end of December 1787 that 'His Majesty the Emperor has now taken me into his service'. Joseph II had appointed him as Court composer in succession to Gluck, who had recently died. But whereas Gluck's salary had been two thousand gulden, Mozart was only paid eight hundred, about £80 a year. His duties were practically non-existent, consisting for the most part of providing dances or light programme music for the Court bands. This was, as he himself wrote, 'too much for what I produce, too little for what I could produce'. When *Don Giovanni* was put on in Vienna, Mozart, knowing that the taste of the capital's public was different from that of the enthusiastic Prague audiences, re-wrote a great part of it, but without achieving success. The Emperor damned it with faint praise, adding, 'No tit-bit for my Viennese!' Following the lead of their Imperial master the Viennese did not like the work.

The current fee for an opera was a down payment of one

hundred gulden. The only way for an eighteenth-century composer to make a bigger profit out of it was to make arrangements of the score for sale to a music publisher. But there was then unfortunately no copyright law to protect him from musical pirates. Leopold had urged Wolfgang to bring out his own arrangement of *The Seraglio* as quickly as possible. Mozart had been at work on a piano arrangement, but was unable to finish it before a pirated version was published in Mainz in 1785.

It would have been more than sufficient to establish the fame and glory of any composer to have written *The Seraglio*, *Figaro*, and *Don Giovanni*. Yet such was Mozart's staggering fertility and facility that, between the first nights of these latter two great operas he had, in a matter of eighteen months, composed thirty-five other works of varying lengths. They include some of his loveliest chamber music, songs, a piano concerto in C, the Prague symphony, the scena and rondo for Nancy Storace, 'Ch'io mi scordi di te', and two of his most beautiful string works, the quintets in C and in G minor, the latter one of the most deeply moving and tragic chamber works ever written.

From the date of production of *Don Giovanni* to that of his next opera, *Così Fan Tutte*, on 26 January 1790 (the eve of his thirty-fourth birthday), he composed a further sixty-three works, including the exquisite clarinet quintet he wrote for his Mannheim friend, Anton Stadler; and within three months, in the summer of 1788, his three last symphonies, the E flat, the G minor, and the C major, called the 'Jupiter' by Salomon, the London impresario, for, as Jupiter reigned supreme among the gods, this symphony was generally regarded as the greatest written at that time. Like his operas, those three symphonies would have made him immortal had he never composed anything else. For he was not 'just' composing. Throughout these later years he was seeking to fuse the galant style of his earlier period with the style of a former day represented by the greatest composer of all time, J. S. Bach. And he succeeded triumphantly in doing so.

From 1788 until 1791 Mozart was producing symphonies, songs, and instrumental music at incredible speed and under feverish pressure, and in this short period he also composed three more operas, including *The Magic Flute*, as well as the *Requiem*, which he did not live to finish. The strain he was putting on himself, however, inevitably affected his health, which was also further weakened by his pitiable financial anxieties. His poverty was not, as has often been said, merely due to his or Constanze's extravagance. There comes a time in the life of all great creative artists when a conflict arises between their need to satisfy their own inner urge for perfection and the necessity to provide for themselves and their families. Mozart had now reached this point of crisis in his creative development. He could no longer trouble merely to tickle or please his public with pretty tunes, and this inevitably destroyed his chances of financial success. He was clearly aware of the situation and was desperately casting around for some means whereby he could resolve his financial problems for a reasonable period.

Mozart had become a Freemason in 1784. As he grew older Freemasonry played an increasingly important part in his spiritual development. It also inspired some of his very greatest music. Benevolence, charity, and brotherly help are fundamental tenets of Freemasonry. And in his distress he now turned to a brother-Mason, Michael Puchberg, for help. Puchberg was both rich and musical and well disposed towards him. On 17 June, 1788, Wolfgang wrote him a letter in which he pathetically described his financial plight, as well as his longing for some security:

> If you have sufficient regard and friendship for me to assist me for a year or two with one or two thousand gulden, at a suitable rate of interest, you will help me enormously! You yourself will surely admit *the sense and truth* of my statement when I say that it is difficult, nay impossible, to live when one has to wait for various odd sums. If one has not at least a *minimum of capital* behind one, it is impossible to keep one's affairs in order. *Nothing* can be done with nothing. If you will do me this kindness then, *primo*, as I shall have some money to go on with, I can meet necessary expenses *whenever they occur*, and therefore *more easily*, whereas now I have to *postpone* payments and then often *at the most awkward time* have to spend *all I receive at one go*; *secondo*, I can work with a mind *more free* from care and *with a lighter heart*, and thus *earn more*.

Perhaps he may have feared that in asking for such a large sum he would receive nothing and, as his situation was really desperate, he continued:

> If you should find it inconvenient to part with so large a sum at once, then I beg you to lend me until to-morrow *at least a couple of hundred* gulden, as my landlord in the Landstrasse has been so importunate that in order to avoid an unpleasant incident I have had to pay him on the spot, and this has made things very awkward for me! We are sleeping to-night, for the first time, in our new quarters, where we shall remain both summer and winter. On the whole the change is all the same to me, in fact I prefer it. As it is, I have very little to do in town and, as I am not exposed to so many visitors, I shall have more time for work. If I have to go to town on business, which will certainly not be very often, any fiacre will take me there for ten kreutzer . . .

As one could have guessed, Puchberg sent the two hundred but not the two thousand gulden, and probably felt himself a very generous fellow for having done so. Had Mozart been able at that stage to find a real backer, he might have lived many more years.

Ten days later an even more pathetic letter followed:

> Vienna, June 27th, 1788
>
> I have been expecting to go to town myself one of these days and to be able to thank you in person for the kindness you have shown me. But now I should not even have the courage to appear before you, as I am obliged to tell you frankly that it is impossible for me to pay back so soon the money you have lent me and that I must beg you to be patient with me! . . . my position is so serious that I am unavoidably obliged to raise money somehow. But, good God, in whom can I confide? . . . I am only too grieved to be in such an extremity; but that is the very reason why I should like a *fairly substantial* sum for a *somewhat longer period*, I mean in order to be able to prevent a recurrence of this state of affairs . . . If my wish is fulfilled, I can breathe freely again, because I shall then be able to put my affairs in order and *keep them so* . . . During the ten days since I came to live here I have done more work than in two months in my former quarters, and if such black thoughts did not come to me so often, thoughts which I banish by a tremendous effort, things would be even better . . .

The work in question, during that summer, consisted of the composition of the three last and greatest symphonies. In the tragic G minor some of those black thoughts are clearly discernible. And it is no paradox that such divine music may have been inspired by such miserable and even sordid cares, but a matter for wonder that this and the other two masterpieces, the E flat and the Jupiter, should have been written in spite of them.

In the spring of 1789 there was a welcome respite. Prince Karl Lichnowsky, one of Mozart's pupils and friends, invited him to go with him to Berlin, where he promised to introduce him to the musical Prussian king, Frederick William II. He naturally accepted this invitation with joyful alacrity. The only drawback to it was the necessity to leave Constanze behind in Vienna. But he nevertheless set forth, at the beginning of April, with relief and hope.

Chapter XI

ICY PREMONITIONS

WOLFGANG'S pleasure in this respite from his debt-ridden and unsuccessful Viennese existence is obvious in all the letters he wrote to his wife during this short trip, which only lasted from April to June 1789, including visits to Prague, Dresden, and to the King of Prussia in Berlin. He wrote eleven letters to Constanze, or, to use his pet-name for her, his 'Stanzerl'. Although four of these letters were lost, the others are among the most enchanting Mozart—or any other husband still in love with his wife after nearly seven years of marriage—ever wrote. In the first one he told her 'not to worry about me, for I am not suffering any discomforts or annoyance on this journey—apart from your *absence*—which as it can't be helped, can't be remedied. I write this note with eyes full of tears.'

He had hoped in Prague to meet some old friends, the singer Frau Duschek and others, but she had already gone on to Dresden, where he shortly rejoined her. 'Dearest little wife! I am simply aching for news of you . . . Kiss our Karl a thousand times.' Constanze and the boy were staying with the Puchbergs, to whom he sent greetings in a postscript, adding in French: 'Adieu, aimez-moi et gardez votre santé si chère et précieuse à votre époux.'

From Dresden he wrote her a long letter on 13 April, containing a delightful observation: 'There was a large party, consisting entirely of ugly women, who by their charm, however, made up for their lack of beauty.' It continues: 'Dearest little wife, if only I had a letter from you! If I were to tell you all the things I do with your dear portrait, I think that you would often laugh. For instance, when I take it out of its case, I say, "Good-day, Stanzerl!—Good-day, little rascal, pussy-pussy, little turned-up nose, little bagatelle, Schluck und Druck", and when I put it away again, I let it slip in very slowly, saying all the time, "Nu-Nu-Nu-Nu!"

with the peculiar *emphasis* which this word so full of meaning demands, and then just at the last, quickly, "Good night, little mouse, sleep well." Well, I suppose I have been writing something very foolish (to the world at all events); but to us who love each other so dearly, it is not foolish at all. Today is the sixth day since I left you and by Heaven! it seems a year.'

The next letter from Dresden followed three days later and was a very long one. After giving her much interesting information about his musical friends and activities there, he told her how, on his return from the opera 'came the happiest of all moments for me. I found a letter from you, that letter which I had longed for so ardently, my darling, my beloved! Madame Duschek and the Neumanns were with me as usual. But I immediately went off in triumph to my room, kissed the letter countless times before breaking the seal, and then devoured it rather than read it. I stayed in my room a long time; for I could not read it or kiss it often enough.'

Nevertheless, this letter had obviously caused him some anxiety as well, for he proceeds to give her a list of requests he has to make:

'(1) not to be melancholy,
(2) *to take care of your health and to beware of the spring breezes,*
(3) not to go out walking alone—and preferably not to *go out walking at all,*
(4) to feel absolutely assured of my love. Up to the present I have not written a single letter to you without placing your dear portrait before me,
(5) and lastly I beg you to send me more details in your letters.'

The final request was rather more than that:

(6) I beg you in your conduct not only to be careful of *your honour and mine*, but also to consider *appearances*. Do not be angry with me for asking this. You ought to love me even more for thus valuing our honour.

And he tactfully mitigated this last paragraph, which might have seemed somewhat admonitory or reproving, by ending:

O Stru! Stri! I kiss and squeeze you 1095060437082 times (now you can practise your pronunciation) and am ever your most faithful husband and friend

W. A. MOZART

A month later he wrote from Leipzig in some distress, for their intervening letters to one another had gone astray. Nevertheless he reminded her to '*Please do all the things I have asked you to do in my letters, for what prompted me was love—real, true love; and love me as I do you.*' Three days later he wrote to tell her that he had arrived in Berlin, and 'trust that you will by now have received some letters from me, for they can't all have been lost . . . Oh, how glad I shall be to be with you again, my darling! But the first thing I shall do is to take you by your front curls; for how on earth could you think, or even imagine, that I had forgotten you? How could I possibly do so? For even *supposing* such a thing you will get on the very first night a thorough spanking.'

On 23 May he wrote again, at great length. Neither of them had apparently had a letter from the other for seventeen days and both were worried. In this one Wolfgang gave Constanze a list of all those he had written to and received from her and promised that '*in your arms* I shall be able to tell you all, all that I felt at that time'. But in this last letter, alas, he also took care to warn her that 'when I return you must be more delighted with having me back than with the money I shall bring. A hundred friedrichs d'or are not nine hundred gulden but seven hundred . . . Secondly, Lichnowsky (as he was in a hurry) left me here, and so I have had to pay for my keep in Potsdam, which is an expensive place. Thirdly, I had to lend him a hundred gulden, as his purse was getting empty. I could not well refuse him: you will know why. Fourthly, my concert at Leipzig was a failure, as I always said it would be, so I had a journey of sixty-four miles there and back almost for nothing . . . But (1) if I gave a concert here I should not make much out of it and (2) the King would not care for me to give one. So you must just be satisfied *as I am with this*, that I am fortunate enough to be enjoying the King's favour.'

Financially this trip had not been the success he had expected. All Mozart got out of it apart from what was left of the seven hundred gulden was a commission to write six string quartets for the King of Prussia and six 'easy' piano sonatas for his daughter. Yet in spite of the failure of his Leipzig concert, he had one supreme thrill in that city, where Johann Sebastian Bach had lived and worked for twenty-five years. Wolfgang met a pupil of his, Johann Friedrich Doles, who had succeeded Bach as Cantor of the famous St Thomas's school. It can be imagined with what rapture Mozart sat down at Bach's organ in St Thomas's church and began to play, and with what amazement old Doles listened to him, for never since Bach's death had he heard anything comparable. In response to Mozart's request, the school choir sang to him one of Bach's motets, 'Sing to the Lord a new song', and at this point the greatest composer of the early eighteenth century and his only true heir in the latter half of it met in musical and spiritual harmony. A very small but also very perfect musical footnote to this profound experience remains to us in the little jig in G, K. 574, in the style of Bach.

2

It is clear from his letters to Constanze during this journey how eagerly he had been looking forward to their reunion. They prove his marital love and need of her, his dependence on her, his frankness in telling her all his troubles and worries and his reliance on her understanding and advice. But he had hardly been home a month when she fell ill and Wolfgang was obliged to turn again to Puchberg for help:

Vienna, July 12th-14th, 1789

Great God! I would not wish my worst enemy to be in my present position. And if you, most beloved friend and brother, forsake me, we are altogether lost, both my *unfortunate and blameless self* and my poor sick wife and child . . . I only dare to write and tremble as I do so—and I should not even dare to write, were I not certain that you know me, that you are aware of my circumstances, and that you are wholly convinced of my *innocence* so far as my unfortunate and most distressing situation is concerned. Good God! I am coming to you not with thanks but with fresh entreaties! Instead of paying my debts I am asking for more money! If you really know me you must sympathize with my anguish in having to do so. I need not tell you once more that owing to my unfortunate illness I have been prevented from earning anything. But I must mention that in spite of my wretched condition I decided to give subscription concerts at home in order to be able to meet at least my present great and frequent expenses, for I was absolutely convinced of your friendly assistance. But even this has failed. Fate is so much against me, *though only in Vienna*, that even when I want to, I cannot make any money. A fortnight ago I sent round a list for subscribers and so far the only name on it is that of Baron van Swieten! Now that (the 13th) my dear little wife seems to be improving every day, I should be able to set to work again, if this blow, this heavy blow, had not come. At any rate, people are consoling me by telling me that she is better—although the night before she was suffering so much—and I on her account—that I was stunned and despairing. But last night (the 14th), she slept so well and has felt so much easier all the morning that I am very hopeful; and at last I am beginning to feel inclined for work. I am now faced, however, with misfortunes of another kind . . .

In this letter Wolfgang alludes to his own ill-health, as well as to Constanze's illness. The strains and stresses of his harassed existence were beginning to tell on him. When he had been in Dresden, a woman artist there, Dora Stock, had made a silver-point drawing of him. In this profile, which was said to be a very good likeness, the wistfulness so characteristic of him is even more evident than usual. Signs of physical weariness are also fairly apparent.

Constanze's illness may have been phlebitis, for her leg was affected. The poor girl was also again pregnant. She was expecting her fifth baby in seven years. She obviously had a strong constitution, since she survived all these pregnancies and the ailments they brought with them and lived until 1842. As Puchberg had not replied to his letter, Wolfgang wrote to him again on 17 July, telling him that Constanze was to take a cure at Baden, and imploring him to help him at once with as much as he could spare, to enable her to go there. Puchberg responded to this appeal with one hundred and fifty gulden, which enabled Mozart to send Constanze away.

The cure must have been extraordinarily rapid and successful, for by the end of August Mozart was again worrying about her, though not with regard to her health. His preoccupation was now the old one—jealousy, and his fear that she was rather too obviously enjoying herself. 'I am glad indeed when you have some fun—of course I am—but I do wish that you would not sometimes make yourself so cheap . . . A woman must always make herself respected or else people will begin to talk about her. My love! Forgive me for being so frank, but my peace of mind demands it as well as our mutual happiness. Remember that you yourself once admitted to me that you were inclined to *comply too easily*. You know the consequences of that. Remember too the promise you gave to me. Oh, God, do try, my love! Be merry and happy and charming to me. Do not torment yourself and me with unnecessary jealousy. Believe in my love, for surely you have proofs of it, and you will see how happy we shall be. Rest assured that it is only by her prudent behaviour that a wife can enchain her husband.'

This letter has often been quoted as evidence that Constanze was unfaithful to her husband. That she was not a 'lady' but a rather 'bohemian', flighty, flirtatious young woman is undeniable. Inevitably, both of them, still so young and high-spirited, were from time to time relieved to escape from their worries and cares, and to enjoy themselves in a brief respite away from them. Since we know that most of the alleged scandalous intrigues Mozart was supposed to have had with other women were merely slanderous inventions by his enemies, one might also give Constanze the benefit of the doubt as regards the accusation that she was not a perfect wife. For no definite evidence of her unfaithfulness exists, and her conduct after Mozart's death seems to confirm the supposition that they were devoted to one another, even if they both occasionally allowed themselves a little fling. The nineteenth century, during which most of this trivially scandalous gossip about their marriage became current, took a much narrower and more reprobatory view of passing flirtations such as they both may have had than either the eighteenth or the twentieth.

Mozart had been unable to accompany Constanze to Baden because it had been decided to revive *The Marriage of Figaro*, which was again performed in Vienna that August. The revival was so successful that it led the Emperor to commission a new Italian opera from his Court composer, who had until then been given nothing much to do except to write a few sets of dance music. Da Ponte was again the librettist, and provided a plot entitled *Così Fan Tutte*, meaning roughly, in English, 'All women are frail by nature'. Da Ponte was a talented librettist but also a slipshod one, always in a hurry, trying to do too many things at once, and a shameless plagiarist. So long as he was adapting a dramatic masterpiece like *Le Mariage de Figaro* or a well-known legend like that of *Don Giovanni*, his weaknesses were not sufficiently blatant to damage their dramatic impact. But in *Così Fan Tutte* they are glaringly revealed.

Two sisters, Fiordiligi and Dorabella, are engaged to two young gallants, Ferrando and Guglielmo. The adoring lovers are quite certain of their girls' fidelity. But Don Alfonso, a cynical old philosopher, declares that all women are naturally unfaithful and sets out to prove this to the two young men. He persuades the lovers to pretend to be called away to war, and to return disguised as a couple of Albanian noblemen. They make love to each other's fiancées, and, after more or less feeble resistance, successfully. The girls' little maid Despina, disguised as a notary, draws up the bogus marriage contracts between the parties. In the end the plot is discovered or unravelled. Don Alfonso has proved his point and the somewhat sobered and disillusioned parties pair off.

Così Fan Tutte is in a way the most controversial of all Mozart's operas. Although the plot provided by Da Ponte is logical and compact within its framework, that framework is utterly cynical, and, unless one accepts its premises, unacceptable. What girl in love would not recognize her own lover, however absurdly disguised; or what couple of mistresses would be deceived for a moment by their own maid in a ridiculous gown and wig? And nowhere in the whole of Mozart's music until then—and indeed after—is there a trace of cynicism, or even in his gayest and most mocking moments anything but sincerity. So here too, he wrote to this crude and uninspiring plot some of his loveliest and most moving music. Certain musicologists have tried to solve the puzzle by suggesting that the whole work should be regarded as a skit, satire, or burlesque, music and all. But to others it seems that the lyrical beauty, passion, and deep seriousness of much of the music is incompatible with the absurdities and unsolved contradictions of the libretto. In *The Seraglio*, Constanze declares in her great aria, 'Martern aller Arten' that in spite of the Pasha's threat of torture she will remain faithful to her fiancé and does so, thereby winning our sympathy and respect. In *Figaro*, the Countess avows in the exquisite 'Dove Sono' her devotion to her unfaithful husband, and captures our hearts. Poor Elvira, in *Don Giovanni*, tells us in 'Mi tradi' that in spite of her seducer's sins against her she still loves him, and we pity her. Pamina, in *The Magic Flute*, is the epitome of beauty and virtue. All these are true Mozartian heroines—brave, tender-hearted women. But in *Così Fan Tutte*, Fiordiligi, who, in her great set-piece, 'Come Scoglio'—('Firm as a rock will I stand') vows fidelity, falls only too easily and forfeits our sympathy. For although, in spite of Da Ponte's cynicism, Mozart gave her such wonderful music to sing, she is out of his line of noble, pure womanhood, which, as so many of his letters to Leopold and Constanze prove, was a deeply personal ideal and the inspiration of some of the loveliest music he wrote.

This opera was first produced on 26 January 1790. During all this time and indeed throughout the year Mozart was in deeper and deeper financial difficulties and continued to assail Puchberg with desperate appeals for help, of which that kind-hearted provider must have been getting pretty sick. Nevertheless he continued to send small sums in response, although by then he must have lost all hope of ever being repaid. And again bad luck supervened.

For Joseph II died within three weeks of the production of *Così Fan Tutte*, and owing to Court mourning all the theatres immediately closed down. By the time of his death his empire was in turmoil and he had alienated all his friends and advisers. His brother and heir, Leopold, Duke of Tuscany, had remained aloof in Italy and only returned to Vienna to ascend the throne.

The new monarch was not a German nationalist, at least, as far as music was concerned. Salieri remained firmly in favour and Mozart was overlooked. But his mercurial temperament never allowed him to refrain from seizing the slightest chance or imagined chance of promotion, and he now persuaded himself, or at any rate attempted to persuade Puchberg, that his prospects were 'now better than ever. I now stand on the threshold of my fortune; but the opportunity will be lost forever, if this time I cannot make use of it.'

This wonderful opportunity consisted in the fact that the post of assistant Court conductor had become vacant; Salieri was conductor-in-chief. It was enough for Mozart to feel, justly, that he had every right to it, for him to assume that he would certainly get it. His Micawberish optimism might seem almost comical had it not been so pathetic and had he not had to point out to Puchberg that 'you know how my present circumstances, were they to become known, would damage the chances of my application to the Court, and how necessary it is that they should remain a secret; for unfortunately at Court they do not judge by circumstances, but solely by appearances. You know, and I am sure you are convinced that if, as I may now confidently hope, my application is successful, you will certainly lose nothing. How delighted I shall be to discharge my debts to you!' The good Puchberg sent another hundred and fifty gulden to enable his poor friend to make a favourable impression. But it was more money wasted, for he did not get the appointment. And if Mozart sponged on Puchberg, he himself was being sponged on, especially by the clarinettist Anton Stadler. Mozart never hesitated to help a fellow artist in distress, although it would no doubt have been much more prudent and sensible of him had he paid off some of his debts instead. In spite of the fact that he was suffering from neuralgia, with constant headaches and toothache, he was composing chamber music, giving private concerts and desperately trying to get new pupils, for he now had only two.

In addition to all this he was also performing a labour of love towards his great predecessor Handel. Baron van Swieten, who had such a keen appreciation of Bach's works, also loved those of Handel. He now introduced Handel's music to Vienna, so many years after it had achieved its tremendous success in London. Van Swieten had arranged some Handel concerts, and when their director, Joseph Starzer, died he asked Mozart to take them over. Mozart borrowed John Mainwaring's *Memoirs of the Life of the Late G. F. Handel* in a German translation from Puchberg, but he had been familiar with his music ever since, as an infant prodigy, he had been asked to play some of it to Queen Charlotte and King George III in London. He reorchestrated Handel's *Acis and Galatea*, parts of *Messiah*, *Alexander's Feast*, and the *Ode on St Cecilia's Day*.

The series of letters appealing to Puchberg for further loans continued throughout April, May, and June of 1790. During the latter month he joined Constanze in Baden, 'For economy's sake . . . and only come into town when it is absolutely necessary' as, on the occasion when he wrote this note, to conduct a performance of *Così Fan Tutte*, which had been revived: 'I have now been obliged to give away my quartets (those very difficult works) for a mere song, simply in order to have cash in hand to meet my present difficulties. I am now composing some piano sonatas.' Puchberg sent a miserable twenty-five gulden this time but can hardly be blamed, considering that by then he must have lent Mozart several hundred.

King Leopold was to be crowned Holy Roman Emperor in Frankfurt-on-Main, on 9 October 1790. The royal suite chosen to accompany him there on that occasion naturally included Salieri and also a German Singspiel composer called Ignaz Umlauff. Mozart was as usual forgotten. In view of all his former failures, his weakening health and his poverty, it seems extraordinary that he should have taken the step on which he now decided. This was to go to Frankfurt at his own expense, taking with him his brother-in-law, Franz Hofer, who had married Constanze's elder sister, Josefa.

Mozart had become completely integrated as a member of the Weber family. He had written many arias for Aloysia, now an established prima donna; her husband, Josef Lange, had painted his portrait. The youngest sister, Sophie, who had married a composer and choir-master called Jakob Haibel, was devoted to Constanze and was with them constantly during Mozart's last illness and at the moment of his death. According to a letter written later by Sophie, Wolfgang had become 'fonder and fonder' of old Frau Weber, to whom he frequently brought little presents of tea and coffee.

Whether Puchberg had refused to advance another loan for the journey, or Mozart was afraid to ask him for one is not on record. But he was confident that with all the festivities in Frankfurt in connection with the coronation, he would be able to give some successful concerts, and so he decided to raise the necessary funds for the journey by pawning his silver plate. He had recovered from his recent bouts of ill-health and set out, as he invariably did, in the highest spirits. His first letter to Constanze from Frankfurt was written with his usual gaiety and optimism. The journey had 'only' taken six days, the weather was lovely, his carriage was splendid. 'At Regensburg we lunched magnificently to the accompaniment of divine music, we had angelic cooking and some glorious Moselle wine.' He had also worked out an excellent plan whereby 'no unforeseen accidents shall ever reduce us to such desperate straits again'. This was to raise two thousand gulden on a draft he was to receive for some compositions from the music publisher Hoffmeister. 'Then everything could be paid off, we should have a little over and on my return I should have nothing to do but work.'

The letters to Constanze on this journey are as loving and devoted as ever but betray a sense of guilt as if she, understandably enough, had been reproaching him for their desperate financial plight. Two days later he wrote to warn her that 'there is no doubt whatever that I shall make something in this place, but certainly not as much as you and some of my friends expect', and at the end of this letter occurs the first whisper of a sinister premonition: 'I am excited as a child at the thought of seeing you again. If people could see into my heart, I should almost feel ashamed. To me everything is cold —cold as ice. Perhaps if you were with me I might possibly take more pleasure in the kindness of those I meet here. But, as it is, everything seems so empty. Adieu, my love. I am ever your husband, who loves you with all his soul.'

The Frankfurt concert took place on 15 October and 'was a splendid success from the point of view of honour and glory, but a failure as far as money was concerned. Unfortunately some Prince was giving a big déjeuner and the Hessian troops were holding a grand manoeuvre. But in any case some obstacle has arisen on every day during my stay here.' The very circumstances from which he had hoped so much, the great social activity connected with the coronation, had ruined his expectations. At this concert, at which in his anxiety for financial as well as artistic success he played as divinely as ever, he performed two concertos, one of which (K. 537) has become known as the 'Coronation' concerto. He left Frankfurt immediately afterwards and returned to Vienna via Mainz, Mannheim, and Munich. They had always loved him in Munich, ever since the production there of *Idomeneo*, and the Elector asked him to appear at a concert which he was giving in honour of the visit of the King of Naples. This king had visited the Emperor in Vienna in the previous month, when works by Salieri, Haydn, and others had been given, but Mozart had been completely passed over. Small wonder that he now wrote bitterly to Constanze: 'It is greatly to the credit of the Viennese Court that the King has to hear me in a foreign country.'

In a previous letter to his wife, on 8 October, 1790, Mozart revealed some of his constant mental worries and perplexities. 'If you could only look into my heart. There is a struggle going on between my yearning and longing to see and embrace you once more and my desire to bring home a large sum of money. I have often thought of travelling *farther afield*, but whenever I tried to bring myself to take the decision, the thought always came to me, how bitterly I should regret it, if I were to separate myself from my beloved wife for *such an uncertain prospect, perhaps even to no purpose whatever*. I feel as if I had left you years ago. Believe me, my love, if you were with me I might perhaps decide more easily, but I am too much accustomed to you and I love you too dearly to endure being separated from you for long.' It was partly for this reason that, when Salomon came to Vienna in the following December, to engage Haydn and Mozart for the London season, Mozart refused the offer on the grounds of other engagements nearer home. Mozart wept when he parted from his dear friend and colleague Haydn, as if that 'icy' premonition had returned, and he knew that he would not see him again.

So London finally missed the chance to welcome him with the rewards given so generously to Handel and Haydn, and Mozart the last opportunity to realize his dream of prosperity and security.

Chapter XII

TAMINO-PAPAGENO

EARLY in the autumn of 1790 Mozart made his twelfth move since his arrival in Vienna nine years previously, to the first floor of a house in the Rauhensteingasse. This was his last home.

His old friend Schikaneder, the touring actor-manager whom he had first met in 1779 during his dreary Salzburg days, had a little theatre in Wieden, a suburb of Vienna. He now persuaded Mozart to compose the music to a German fairy-tale opera he was planning to put on there. It was to be called *Die Zauberflöte—The Magic Flute*. Mozart was not at first too keen to do it. But he was harder up than ever, and Constanze, who was again pregnant, was spending the summer in Baden. In the previous May he had applied to the Municipal Council of Vienna for the post of unpaid assistant to their conductor and organist Leopold Hofman, who was then sixty-one and ill, in the hope of succeeding him when he died. But Hofman recovered and outlived him.

During that summer Mozart himself was very run down and, as usual, overworking. His output during this last year of his life was staggering. It included two operas, *The Magic Flute* and *La Clemenza di Tito*, a mass of chamber music and Masonic cantatas, the motet *Ave, Verum Corpus*, and even music for mechanical instruments and dances for the Court. He suffered, also as usual, from Constanze's absence, and worried about his little boy, Karl, who was boarded out at school.

In order to enable him to work in pleasant open-air sur-roundings, Schikaneder installed him in a little summer-house or pavilion near his theatre. He and the cast kept Mozart company from time to time and held gay parties to help raise his spirits. These, like every attempt he made to amuse or dis-tract himself, were immediately described as drunken orgies by his still vigilant enemies. But as the company included his sister-in-law, Josefa Hofer (who was to sing the Queen of the

Night in the first production of *The Magic Flute*) these rumours were probably more scandalous than accurate. He wrote to Constanze nearly every day and went to stay with her in Baden whenever he could do so. All his letters expressed his longing for her, for he could not bear to be parted from her, nor to work or sleep alone. He stayed for part of the time with an old friend, Joseph Leutgeb, who had been a horn-player in the Salzburg orchestra but since 1777 had lived in Vienna, where he had gone into trade as a cheesemonger. It was for him that Mozart wrote his delightful Horn Quintet K. 407 in 1784. Wolfgang ate his meals in the 'Ungarische Krone'—the Hungarian Crown—and wandered rather miserably from there to one or the other coffee-house, looking for companionship.

> Vienna, June 12th, 1791
>
> . . . In the evening I again took a meal at the 'Krone' simply in order not to be alone, and there at least I found someone to talk to. Then I went straight to bed. I was up again at five o'clock . . .

> Vienna, July 17th, 1791
>
> . . . You cannot imagine how I have been aching for you all this long while. I can't describe what I have been feeling— a kind of emptiness, which hurts me dreadfully—a kind of longing, which is never satisfied, which never ceases, and which persists, nay rather increases daily . . . Even my work gives me no pleasure, because I am accustomed to stop working now and then and exchange a few words with you. Alas! this pleasure is no longer possible. If I go to the piano and sing something out of my opera, I have to stop at once, for this stirs my emotions too deeply. Basta! The very hour after I finish this business I shall be off and away from here . . .

Nevertheless he wrote gaily as well, with his usual sense of fun, teasing her and his pupil Süssmayr, who was staying part of the time with Constanze in Baden. During the last six months of Wolfgang's life Franz Süssmayr became an indispensable member of the Mozart household. He had originally joined Mozart in order to study composition with him, but during this final period he became his closest collaborator and amanuensis. These last little notes and letters to Constanze contain charming gleams of the gaiety and humour, the affectionate

nonsense, so characteristic of Wolfgang's earlier correspondence:

> . . . Think of me and talk about me very often, both of you.
> Love me for ever as I do you and be always my Stanzi Marini,
> as I shall always be your
>
> Stu! Knaller Praller
> Schnip-Schnap-Schnur
> Schnepeperl—
> Snai!—
>
> Give N.N. (Süssmayr) a box on the ear and tell him that
> you simply must kill a fly which I have spied on his . . . face!
> Adieu—Look there! Catch them—bi—bi—bi three kisses, as
> sweet as sugar, are flying over to you!
> Wednesday, Vienna, July 6th, 1791.

Later that month Constanze returned to Vienna, where she
was delivered of their sixth and last child on 26 July, another
boy, whom they called Franz Xaver Wolfgang.

During July there also occurred a mysterious and somewhat
macabre incident. An unknown man soberly cloaked in grey
knocked at the door one evening and presented Mozart with
an anonymous letter. In this he was invited to compose a
Requiem Mass at any figure he himself chose to charge for
doing so. The matter was to be regarded as confidential and
kept strictly secret. Mozart was unable to glean any further
information from the stranger, who merely requested, very
politely, an answer: Yes or No? He was in no position to refuse
any commission and therefore agreed to write the *Requiem*, for
the price of fifty ducats. This sum was duly paid and he was
promised the same amount on delivery. Again it was stressed
that the commission must remain a dead secret.

Having agreed to this unusual proposition, Mozart continued to work on *The Magic Flute* and nearly forgot about his
new commitment, the more so because almost immediately
afterwards, in August, his friends in Prague, who had always
remained loyal to him and to his work, sought him out with an
even more urgent demand. The Emperor Leopold II was to be
crowned King of Bohemia there on 6 September, and the
Prague authorities had suddenly decided to stage an opera in
honour of this event, which they now—only a few weeks in
advance of it—asked Mozart to compose for them. Once again

the opportunity was too good a one to miss and he accepted the invitation, which meant dropping all his work on *The Magic Flute* and rushing off to Prague with Constanze, fortunately with Süssmayr in attendance.

As they were all three about to enter their carriage the mysterious man in grey suddenly appeared as from nowhere, and tapping Mozart on the shoulder, reminded him of his promise to write the *Requiem*. This unexpected reappearance of the stranger brought back with a rush all those icy premonitions from which Wolfgang had been suffering. Hurriedly he promised to fulfil his bargain, but he could not shake off a feeling of dread and depression for the whole of the journey.

There was, however, no time to give way to it. He began instantly to compose *La Clemenza di Tito*, as the Prague opera was called, and at every halt he would sit up all night working at it, with Süssmayr's help. Nor was this subject very much to his taste. The libretto which had been decided upon was an old one of Metastasio's, which had been re-arranged for this occasion, a dreary story in the *opera seria* style to which he had not returned since *Idomeneo*. Occupied as his mind still was with *The Magic Flute*, which was to express so perfectly all his modern musical ideas, the fusion of the old and the new German styles which it was triumphantly to embody, he could not now at short notice successfully revert to the old-fashioned Italian forms. In spite of the fact (or perhaps because of it) that the opera was written and rehearsed in three weeks, and produced with costly settings and costumes after the coronation banquet, it was an utter failure. The Empress dismissed it contemptuously as 'just another German piggery'. In our time the overture is performed fairly frequently, but the full work comparatively rarely.

On their return from Prague Constanze went back to Baden to recover from her last pregnancy, whilst Wolfgang plunged into the final effort of completing *The Magic Flute*. Its importance in his creative life can only be understood by a short discussion of the libretto and the music. The plot was devised by Schikaneder and one of his chorus singers, C. L. Giesecke. Schikaneder, in the true theatrical tradition, was only interested in providing himself with a superb comic star part, that of the 'gentle savage', the simple bird-catcher Papageno.

Giesecke, however, was a remarkably versatile character, whose biography is extraordinarily romantic.

His real name was Johann Georg Metzler. He was born in Augsburg—Leopold Mozart's birthplace—and studied law at the University of Göttingen. But his chief bent seems to have been scientific, for he became a famous mineralogist. Three years after the first production of *The Magic Flute* he set out on his travels and spent some time in Denmark, opening a school of mineralogy in Copenhagen in 1806. The King, Christian VII, enabled him to go on an exploratory expedition to Greenland, where he remained for more than seven years, collecting masses of mineralogical specimens. He returned, not to Denmark but to England, and landed at Hull, in August 1813, 'looking', as Dent picturesquely wrote, 'probably rather like Papageno, for his European clothes had worn out and he was dressed as an Eskimo in fur and feathers. He was given a hearty welcome . . . and in December of that year was elected to the Royal Dublin Society's . . . professorship of mineralogy'. Later a knighthood was conferred on him. He became Sir Charles Lewis Giesecke and was painted in 1817 by Raeburn.

But in 1791 the most important thing about Giesecke was the fact that he, like Mozart and Schikaneder (and indeed most of the leading intellectuals of the time) was an enthusiastic Freemason.

The Magic Flute, to outward appearance merely an innocuous and occasionally absurd fairy-tale or pantomime, is in fact a unique example of operatic 'double-talk'. It is unmistakably what we nowadays call propaganda, with a clear message standing for truth, reason, and wisdom against superstition and intolerance.

Tamino, a young prince astray in a foreign, pseudo-Egyptian land, is requested by the Queen of the Night to rescue her lovely daughter Pamina from a wicked sorcerer called Sarastro, who has kidnapped her. With him goes, as a kind of retainer, a bird-catcher, Papageno. Her ladies-in-waiting give Tamino a magic flute to protect him, and Papageno a glockenspiel, or set of bells. But Tamino's illusions gradually fade, as he discovers that he has been deluded by the Queen of the Night and that Sarastro, the benevolent leader of a priestly order, has in fact rescued Pamina for her own good from her mother, a malevolent witch. After enduring various trials, modelled by Giesecke largely on the probationary rites of the Masonic order, Tamino and Pamina are united. But the final triumph is more than the conventional one of hero and heroine; it also symbolizes and proclaims the triumph of universal love and the brotherhood of man.

These mystical rites and vows inspired some of Mozart's grandest music. They are paralleled or, rather, parodied, in the case of Papageno, who, to the sparkling sounds of his magic bells, also wins through and gains a little bird-wife, Papagena. Their delightful duet in the opera's penultimate scene invariably brings down the house.

Many modern opera-goers, although they find the music entrancing, complain that the libretto seems nonsensical. 'Why?' they ask, 'the magic flute? It's very pretty, but what has it to do with the story?' The answer is: 'Everything. The Flute *is*, in fact, the story.'

Originally this opera, a Singspiel, contained a great deal more dialogue that was not set to music by Mozart, but without a knowledge of which the plot is not easily comprehensible. The original version makes it clear beyond doubt that the Queen of the Night is the widow of Sarastro's predecessor in the Order, and that on her husband's death she had considered herself his rightful successor. According to the rules, however, a woman could not succeed to this position of leadership, and the Shield of the Sun, symbol of power, had been given into Sarastro's keeping. But the Queen still possessed one magic weapon, the Flute, which, as Pamina at the end tells Tamino: 'from mystic tree was carven, And round it mighty spells were woven; the sacred bough *my father* tore, Nor feared the lightnings' thunderous roar.' The Queen sent this Magic Flute to Tamino as a powerful talisman against Sarastro. In order to further her plot to overthrow the new leader of the Order she had hidden herself and her ladies in the subterranean halls of the temple, only emerging at night. But Sarastro, wiser than the Queen, had taken her daughter Pamina under his care with the intention of making her the wife of the young man (Tamino) worthy to be in due course elected to succeed himself, when the succession would be (and at the end is) once more re-established. With the Magic Flute and under the

Shield of the Sun, Tamino is confirmed as Sarastro's heir, and Pamina as his partner and guide, 'as', she tells him, 'love is guide for me'.

The first Tamino, incidentally, was an accomplished flautist as well as a tenor—the only one who actually played the flute in addition to singing the part.

Had *The Magic Flute* not contained a great deal of gay nonsense and 'effects' introduced by Schikaneder it would on its original production almost certainly have run up against the censorship of the day. Amongst its more obviously harmless fooling it undoubtedly represented to its contemporaneous Viennese audiences as pointed a political satire as *Figaro*, and a more daring one, for it was both anti-monarchical and anti-clerical. They interpreted Sarastro's declaration of war on the Queen of the Night and 'degraded superstition' as referring to their late Queen, Maria Theresa, whilst the blackamoor Monastatos, who joins forces with her when driven out of the Temple, was to them a symbol of clerical despotism.

The great conductor Bruno Walter wrote of this work: 'At last, in *The Magic Flute*, he opened his lips and poured out his heart in the tones and words of Sarastro and Tamino; and in the proclamations of the former the world may recognize Mozart's own spiritual will and testament . . . And maybe to-day more than ever Mozart's music proves its helpful, blessing power on those to whom it speaks.'

Whilst Tamino embodies all Mozart's noblest aspirations and thoughts, the charming but naughty Papageno represents his lower nature. (In Freudian terms they symbolize his ego and his id.) This duality in his character as well as in his music reveals itself frequently in Mozart's correspondence, both with his father and his wife, and the 'Bäserl' letters of his youth are the most typical expression we have of the Papageno side of his nature.

The *Flute* was first produced on 30 September 1791, with Mozart conducting it from the harpsichord. His health had not improved and he was so depressed on the first night that he had to be dragged on by Schikaneder to take his call. He seems, however, to have recovered his spirits very rapidly. Constanze had returned to Baden and from his letters to her during October it is clear what great happiness Mozart was enjoying as the result of *The Magic Flute*'s success, which very quickly established itself in public favour:

> Vienna, October 7th-8th, 1791
> Friday, half past ten at night
> . . . You can see how this opera is becoming more and more popular. Now for an account of my own doings. Immediately after your departure I played two games of billiards with Herr von Mozart, the fellow who wrote the opera which is running at Schikaneder's theatre; then I sold my nag for fourteen ducats; then I told Joseph (his servant) to get Primus to fetch me some black coffee, with which I smoked a splendid pipe of tobacco; and then I orchestrated almost the whole of Stadler's rondo.[1]

Mozart seems at this time to have been in very good health, and in true Papageno style gave Constanze details of his excellent appetite and the succulent meals he was enjoying, cutlets on Friday, and on Saturday night 'I have just swallowed a delicious slice of sturgeon which Don Primus (who is my faithful valet) has brought me; and as I have rather a voracious appetite to-day, I have sent him off again to fetch some more if he can . . . This morning I worked so hard at my composition that I went on until half-past one. So I dashed off in great haste to Hofer, simply in order not to lunch alone, where I found Mamma too. After lunch I went home at once and composed again until it was time to go to the opera . . . I am taking *Mamma* tomorrow. Hofer has already given her the libretto to read. In her case what will probably happen will be that she will *see* the opera, but not *hear* it.'

The most endearing passage in this letter, however, is Mozart's account of the prank he played that night on Schikaneder, who was, of course, appearing as Papageno. 'But during Papageno's aria with the glockenspiel I went behind the scenes, as I felt a sort of impulse to-day to play it myself. Well, just for fun, at the point where Schikaneder has a pause, I played an *arpeggio*. He was startled, looked behind the wings and saw me. When he had his next pause, I played no *arpeggio*. This time he stopped and refused to go on. I guessed what he

---

[1] This Rondo was the last movement of his exquisite clarinet concerto, which ever since has been played by every great clarinettist the world over.

was thinking and again played a chord. He then struck the glockenspiel and said "*Shut up*". Whereupon everyone laughed. I am inclined to think that this joke taught many of the audience for the first time that Papageno does not play the instrument himself.' (Mamma was, of course, Frau Weber, who was presumably rather deaf by then.)

On 14 October, her son-in-law again took the old lady to *The Magic Flute* and also 'I called in the carriage for Salieri and Madame Cavalieri—and drove them to my box . . . You can hardly imagine how charming they were and how much they liked not only my music, but the libretto and everything. They both said that it was an *operone* (a grand opera) worthy to be performed for the grandest festival and before the greatest monarch, and that . . . they had never seen a more beautiful or delightful show. Salieri listened and watched most attentively and from the overture to the last chorus there was not a single number that did not call forth from him a bravo! or a bello!'

Was Salieri sincere, or was this merely hypocrisy on his part, by which Wolfgang, in his simplicity and professional pride, was completely taken in? For Salieri, the leading Court composer to Joseph II and Leopold II, was Mozart's chief rival and most embittered opponent. For years after Mozart's death the legend persisted that Salieri had poisoned him, so that on his death-bed in 1825 the old composer, then seventy-five, once again had to deny the accusation. (The Russian poet Pushkin wrote a play on this theme, and the composer Rimsky-Korsakov based an opera on it, entitled *Mozart and Salieri*.) There is no doubt that Salieri was not guilty of poisoning poor Wolfgang in a physical sense; but it is equally true that for years he did poison the Viennese atmosphere against him, although he was certainly not the only one of Mozart's vile detractors. Mozart was accused of the wildest extravagance and profligacy; his debts were said to amount to thousands of gulden. The story was spread that he was a drunkard and an unfaithful husband. But Wolfgang's last letters to Constanze reveal him in a very different light. He was always struggling to take care of her and their children. His last letter of all—she returned from Baden shortly afterwards—shows how keenly aware he was of his responsibilities as a father, and that he was doing his very best to cope with them:

Karl was absolutely delighted at being taken to the opera. He is looking splendid. As far as health is concerned, he could not be in a better place, but everything else is wretched, alas! . . . As his serious studies (God help them!) do not begin until Monday, I have arranged to keep him until after lunch on Sunday. I told them that you would like to see him. So to-morrow, Saturday, I shall drive out with Karl to see you. You can then keep him, or I shall take him back to Heeger's after lunch. Think it over. A month can hardly do him much harm. In the meantime the arrangement with the Piarists, which is now under discussion, may come to something . . .

For Mozart was anxious that the boy should receive a good education and was trying to place him in the school of the Piarist fathers:

On the whole Karl is no worse; but at the same time he is not one whit better than he was. He still has his old bad manners; he never stops chattering just as he used to do in the past; and he is, if anything, *less inclined to learn than before*, as out at Perchtholdsdorf all he does is to run about in the garden for five hours in the morning and five hours in the afternoon, as he himself confessed.

This letter might well have been written by Leopold. It shows very touchingly how hard Wolfgang was trying to bring up his own son according to his father's firm and pious tradition.

Chapter XIII

DEATH

No opera ever written has a more tragic last act than Mozart's death. Leopold had often boasted of his own ability to foresee events correctly, a kind of intuition or extra-sensory perception. And now it seemed as if Wolfgang had the same gift. The commission to write the *Requiem* and the mysterious circumstances surrounding it appeared to him like an uncanny warning from the unseen. He became convinced that he was writing it for himself.

At about the time that the mysterious man in grey had paid his first call on him Wolfgang was feeling physically ill, and the psychological shock caused by this strange visit increased his misery. He imagined that someone had tried to poison him with a substance called *acqua toffana*. Poisoning was then still a fairly common form of murder. The substance Mozart thought had been secretly given him was invented by a Neapolitan woman called Tofana, and was first brought to public notice in Rome in 1659, when a group of ladies whose husbands had died too suddenly and inexplicably attracted the attention of the local police.

If at this time poor Mozart had delusions of persecution it is hardly surprising. Nevertheless they were delusions. For whatever he did die from—and various theories have been brought forward to explain his symptoms—his death appears to have been a natural one.

This story of his fear that he had been poisoned was told by Constanze to Vincent and Mary Novello, who visited her at Salzburg in July 1829. Each of them separately made notes of their conversations with her. Mary was a less sentimental reporter than Vincent and records Constanze's description of it as follows:

> M.N. (July 17th) Some six months before his death he was possessed with the idea of his being poisoned—'I know I must die', he exclaimed, 'someone has given me acqua toffana and

has calculated the precise time of my death—for which they have ordered a Requiem, it is for myself I am writing this'. His wife entreated him to let her put it aside, saying that he was ill, otherwise he would not have such an absurd idea. He agreed she should and wrote a masonic ode which so delighted the company for whom it was written that he returned quite elated: 'Did I not know that I have written better I should think this the best of my work, but I will put it in score. Yes, I see I was ill to have had such an absurd idea of having taken poison, give me back the Requiem and I will go on with it.' But in a few days he was as ill as ever and possessed with the same idea.[1]

But if this fixation that he had been poisoned was a symptom that his illness was affecting his mind, and (as was the case) the commission to write the *Requiem* can be explained in perfectly simple and non-supernatural terms, the fact nevertheless remains that it was the last work Mozart ever wrote, that he died leaving it unfinished, and that therefore his premonitions of death, although based on no rational grounds, were correct. Nor did he live long enough to know the identity of the stranger in grey and the use to which his *Requiem* was meant to be put.

The facts only emerged after his death. A certain Austrian aristocrat bearing the title of Count Franz von Walsegg zu Stuppach had a musical bee in his bonnet. He used in secret to buy or commission works from professional composers and then have them performed at his private concerts, where he passed them off on his friends as his own unaided efforts. A ridiculous but harmless eccentricity had he not commissioned the *Requiem*, which he wanted to have performed in memory of his late wife, from Mozart, and by doing so given his eccentricity a macabre twist. He himself was not the messenger in the grey cloak. This was a neighbour of von Walsegg's called Anton von Leitgeb, who was in his confidence and carried out the commission on Walsegg's behalf.

Mozart went on working at the *Requiem*, but by the middle of November 1791 was so ill that he had to be put to bed. He had the score constantly with him and continued to compose whenever he felt able to do so. Süssmayr hardly ever left him and gave him a great deal of help. According to Mary

---

[1] *A Mozart Pilgrimage*, by Nerina Medici and Rosemary Hughes, p. 125.

Novello's report, on the days when he felt better Constanze, Süssmayr, and Wolfgang would sing parts of it over together.

On 7 April 1825 his sister-in-law, Sophie, who of her three sisters was the closest to Constanze and extremely devoted to her and Mozart, wrote a letter describing his last hours. It was an intimate 'family' letter, written many years later, with no stylistic pretensions at all, and is all the more touching on that account:

Diakovar, April 7th, 1825

Now I must tell you about Mozart's last days . . . when Mozart fell ill, we both (Sophie and his mother-in-law, old Frau Weber) made him a night-jacket which he could put on frontways, since on account of his swollen condition he was unable to turn in bed . . . I used to go into town every day to see him. Well, one Saturday when I was with him, Mozart said to me: 'Dear Sophie, do tell Mamma that I am fairly well and that I shall be able to go and congratulate her on the octave of her name-day.' . . . I hurried home therefore to comfort her, the more so as he himself really seemed to be bright and happy. The following day was a Sunday . . . But I never cared to go out walking from our suburb into town in my fine clothes, and I had no money for a drive. So I said to our good mother: 'Dear Mamma, I'm not going to see Mozart to-day. He was so well yesterday that . . . one day more or less won't make much difference.' Well, my mother said: '. . . Make me a bowl of coffee and then I'll tell you what you ought to do.' . . . I went into the kitchen. The fire was out. I had to light the lamp and make a fire. All the time I was thinking of Mozart. I had made the coffee and the lamp was still burning . . . It was still burning brightly. I stared into the flame and thought to myself, 'How I should love to know how Mozart is.' While I was thinking and gazing at the flame it went out, as completely as if the lamp had never been burning. Not a spark remained on the main wick and yet there wasn't the slightest draught—that I can swear to. A horrible feeling came over me. I ran to our mother and told her all. She said: 'Well, take off your fine clothes and go into town and bring me back news of him at once. But be sure not to delay.' I hurried along as fast as I could. Alas, how frightened I was when my sister, who was almost despairing and yet trying to keep calm, came out to me, saying: 'Thank God that you have come, dear Sophie. Last night he was so ill that I thought he would not be alive this morning. Do stay with me to-day, for if he has another bad turn, he will pass away to-night. Go in to him for a little while and see how he is.' I tried to control myself and went to his bedside. He immediately called me to him and said: 'Ah, dear Sophie, how glad I am that you have come. You must stay here to-night and see me die.' I tried hard to be brave and to persuade him to the contrary. But to all my attempts he only replied: 'Why, I am already tasting death. And, if you do not stay, who will support my dearest Constanze when I am gone?' 'Yes, yes, dear Mozart,' I assured him, 'but I must first go back to our mother and tell her that you would like me to stay with you to-day. Otherwise she will think that some misfortune has befallen you.' 'Yes, do so,' said Mozart, 'but be sure and come back soon.' Good God! how distressed I felt! My poor sister followed me to the door and begged me for Heaven's sake to go to the priests at St Peter's and implore one of them to come to Mozart—a chance call, as it were. I did so, but for a long time they refused to come and I had a great deal of trouble to persuade one of those heartless people to go to him. Then I ran off to my mother who was anxiously awaiting me. It was already dark. Poor soul, how shocked she was! I persuaded her to go and spend the night with her eldest daughter, the late Josefa Hofer. I then ran back as fast as I could to my distracted sister. Süssmayr was at Mozart's bedside. The well-known Requiem lay on the quilt and Mozart was explaining to him how, in his opinion, he ought to finish it, when he was gone. Further, he urged his wife to keep his death a secret until she should have informed Albrechtsberger, who was in charge of all the services. A long search was made for Dr Closset, who was found at the theatre, but who had to wait for the end of the play. He came and ordered cold poultices to be placed on Mozart's burning head, which, however, affected him to such an extent that he became unconscious until he died. His last movement was an attempt to express with his mouth the drum passages in the Requiem. That I can still hear. Müller from the Art Gallery came and took a case of his pale, dead face. Words fail me, dearest brother, to describe how his wife in her utter misery threw herself on her knees and implored the Almighty for His aid. She simply could not tear herself away from Mozart, however much I begged her to do so. If it were possible to increase her sorrow, this was done on the day after that distressing night, when crowds of people walked past his corpse and wept and mourned for him. All my life I have never seen Mozart in a temper, still less angry.

Mozart died at five minutes to one on 6 December, 1791.

Even on his death-bed he was thinking of others. When he told Constanze to keep his death a secret until she should have informed Albrechtsberger of it, he was anxious that, as he would not live to succeed Hofman as organist at St Stephen's, Albrechtsberger should be the first to know this, so that he might immediately apply for the appointment. He did so and received it.

When he died Mozart also had other prospects, offers both from Hungary and from Holland, and Salomon had been most anxious to engage him for London. But his fortunes turned too late, and he knew it. According to Niemetschek ' "Just now", thus he often complained in his illness, "when I could have gone on living so peacefully, I must depart. I must leave my art now that I am no longer a slave of fashion, am no longer tied to speculators; when I could follow the paths along which my spirit leads me, free and independent to write only when I am inspired. I must leave my family, my poor children, just when I would have been in a better position to look after their welfare." '[1]

Mozart's death was tragic, but his burial was fantastic. The facts about his funeral and the disposal of his body became encrusted with legends, both absurd and macabre. Constanze broke down completely and was taken away from Wolfgang's death-bed by friends. In any case women did not usually attend funerals. The arrangements were made by Baron van Swieten, who ordered the cheapest possible funeral, to save the family expenses they could not afford. After a short open-air service at St Stephen's—for only better-class services were held inside the church—the body of Mozart (who had so loved fine carriages) was placed in a miserable hearse for its journey to the graveyard, some distance from the town. A few of his friends, including, apparently, Süssmayr, van Swieten, and Salieri, followed it on foot. It is not known for certain who they were, as none of them left a personal statement on the subject. They accompanied the hearse as far as the city gates and then it

[1] *Life of Mozart*, by Franz Niemetschek, pp. 45-6.

trundled on alone, without a single mourner to accompany it. The coffin was delivered to the grave-digger at the burial ground of St Mark's, who, lacking any instruction to the contrary, was presumed to have dumped it into a common grave. Not until a very long time afterwards did anyone trouble to find out what had become of the body. But by then it was too late to recover it.

And that was the end of the mortal remains of Wolfgang Amadeus Mozart, aged thirty-five years and eleven months.

Some sixty years later an article appeared in a Viennese newspaper in which one of the alleged mourners explained the apparent defection of Mozart's friends as due to a violent storm, which drenched them, and from which they sought refuge in a local inn. It was not until 1960 that this explanation—which no member of his family, nor Nissen, in his biography, had supported—was revealed as entirely mythical. In 1959 a musicologist, Nicolas Slonimsky, had the simple but bright idea of applying to the Vienna *Zentralanstalt für Meteorologie* to inquire whether any records existed with reference to the weather in Vienna on 6 December 1791. He received a prompt reply from the director, Professor F. Steinhauser, that such records did exist, proving conclusively that on that date there was no storm of any kind. The meteorological records were further confirmed by the diary of a contemporary, Count Karl Zinzendorf, in which under the date of 6 December the Count had noted that the weather was mild and foggy.[1]

Professor Steinhauser further explained that 'in the eighteenth century it was customary to accompany the body to the grave only when the cemetery was situated in the immediate vicinity of the church'.

The fact remains, nevertheless, that the disposal of Mozart's body and the site where it was interred are still a mystery.

2

Mozart left two hundred gulden in cash—about £20—and his furniture and effects were valued at another two hundred. His debts amounted to about £300, a third of which Puchberg had advanced. He, good man, did not press Constanze for

---

[1] Nicolas Slonimsky, 'The Weather at Mozart's Funeral', *The Musical Quarterly* (January 1960.)

payment and even took charge of the two little orphans, Karl, aged seven, and the baby, Franz Xaver, until she was well enough to look after them.

Almost as soon as Constanze had recovered from the shock of Mozart's death, she seems to have behaved with great dignity and was regarded with respect by all his friends. One of her most pressing problems was the unfinished *Requiem*, for which Mozart had been promised another fifty gulden on delivery, money she now desperately needed. She asked various of his colleagues to complete it, fearing that if this were not done she might even have to repay the fifty gulden already received for it. But none of them would do so. Finally the devoted Süssmayr stepped into the breach. He carried out his task as faithfully as his memory of his master's intentions permitted. The *Requiem* was then delivered—and paid for—as Mozart's. This was no doubt a somewhat dishonest transaction. But Count von Walsegg himself was hardly in a position to throw stones into Constanze's glass-house, considering that he had intended to pass it off as his own original work. When the *Requiem* was in due course performed at a benefit concert for Mozart's widow and children, this exposure of his attempted fraud must have been unpleasant for him.

The Emperor Leopold II died early in the following spring after a very short reign, and was succeeded in March 1792 by his son, who became the Emperor Francis II. He too had known Mozart for many years. Her friends now advised Constanze to seek an audience with him. He received her benevolently and gave her an opportunity to tell him the truth about Mozart's life and death, to refute the lies and slanders that had so wickedly been put about by his enemies. He awarded her a small pension, and gave his patronage to the concert.

It seems incredible today, but when Mozart died only about one hundred and fifty of his six to seven hundred works had been published. After his death Constanze supported herself and her children by following the example of her mother, old Frau Weber, who had died in 1793. She let rooms. In 1797 one of her lodgers was a Danish diplomat, Georg Nikolaus van Nissen, Secretary to the Danish Legation. He helped her to sell some of Mozart's manuscripts to Breitkopf and Härtel, the music publishers.

Another good friend also helped. In December 1787 Joseph Haydn had written to a friend in Prague: 'For if I were to make as lasting an impression on music lovers, particularly the eminent ones, as Mozart's inimitable works have done, nations would compete to possess such a treasure within their boundaries. Prague must hold on to this precious man, but he must also have recompense, for without that, the story of men of great talent is sad indeed, and gives those who come after, little encouragement to make further efforts. For lack of this, unfortunately, so many who began in hope have succumbed. I am simply furious that this unique Mozart has not yet been engaged by an Imperial or Royal Court.

'Pardon my wandering from the subject—Mozart is a man very dear to me.'[1]

When Haydn heard of his beloved Mozart's death, and his widow's poverty, he suggested to a young music publisher, Anton André, that he should buy some of Mozart's unpublished scores from Constanze. At his death his manuscripts were in a chaotic condition, and Constanze was unable to make a list of them unaided. She was helped, however, by one of his old friends, the Abbé Stadler (not related to the sponging clarinettist) and in her business negotiations with the publishers by Nissen.

Mozart himself had kept a list of his compositions as he wrote them from 1784 till his death, but the earlier works were not included in this. An authoritative catalogue was not made until the middle of the nineteenth century, when a musician called Ludwig von Köchel undertook this difficult and important task. It is usual for the works of a composer to be listed in chronological order, according to the dates of composition or 'opus' numbers. But in Mozart's case such a complete catalogue did not exist until Köchel made it, and Mozart's compositions have ever since been classified under the initial K, followed by the number assigned to each one by Köchel.

It is not known whether Nissen married Mozart's widow in 1809 because of his passion for her first husband's music, or whether it was inspired by her. Although not born a lady,

---

[1] Niemetschek, *Life of Mozart*, pp. 60-1.

Constanze now became one by marriage, and spent ten years in Copenhagen with her second husband.

A portrait of Constanze painted by Hans Hansen in 1802, holding, presumably, a manuscript of one of Mozart's compositions, shows that at the age of thirty-nine she was still an attractive and intelligent-looking woman. Her hair-style appears to be singularly in the fashion of our own time. She still had the pretty little dark curls over her forehead that Wolfgang had so loved to tweak when teasing her. Her black eyes have a slightly cold expression and the set of her lips and chin shows evidence of a firm and decided character. In this portrait she looks like a very practical and even astute business woman. Much as Mozart had loved her, she had had a hard and difficult life with him, and a series of pregnancies that had undermined her health during most of her youth. There is little evidence that their financial difficulties were altogether her fault and, according to Mozart's letters, during their engagement she made most of her own clothes. She may not at first have been deeply in love with him. He was, after all, her successful elder sister's cast-off lover, and Constanze probably had no other suitor. But no one can read his letters and remain for an instant in doubt that Wolfgang loved her more and more as time went on, and that whatever her faults may have been, she gave him many hours of joy and happiness.

On his retirement in 1820, Nissen and Constanze settled in Salzburg, Mozart's birthplace. Nissen, with Constanze's help, was writing Mozart's first full-length biography. Sophie's letter describing Wolfgang's last hours was written to Nissen in 1825. He himself died in the following year, 1826, before the biography appeared. Constanze saw it through the press and published it in 1828. After Sophie was also widowed she joined her sister in Salzburg. By this time Mozart's fame and legend had begun to spread all over Europe.

Mozart's two surviving sons were both musical. Karl did not become a professional musician, although he was a good pianist. In 1798 he went to Italy, where he was apprenticed to a business man in Leghorn. He remained in that country, becoming an Austrian government official in Milan. He died there, unmarried, in 1858.

Franz Xaver Wolfgang was later known as Wolfgang

Amadeus Mozart the second. He did make music his career and appears to have had considerable talent, both as executant and composer. Vincent and Mary Novello met him when they visited Constanze in Salzburg in July 1829. Vincent wrote: 'Young Mozart is a melancholy thoughtful-looking Person—he is short and rather stout, with very frank, and unaffected, quiet manners, his face somewhat resembling his Father's, especially the forehead. He is (*unfortunately*, I think) a Professor of Music, and seems to be impressed with the idea, that everything he can possibly do, will be so greatly inferior to what was accomplished by the wonderful genius of his illustrious father, that he feels disinclined to write much, or to publish what he produces.'[1]

Franz Xaver lived in Lemberg, where he composed, conducted and taught. He also made one or two concert tours. Like his brother he died a bachelor, in 1844. Wolfgang's fate was tragic, but Franz Xaver's was pathetic. It was one that has been shared by other sons of men of genius, hopelessly overshadowed from birth by their fathers' reputations.

There was another still more pathetic member of the Mozart family living in Salzburg in 1829. Vincent Novello had heard that Mozart's sister, the Baroness zu Sonnenburg, was then in very straitened circumstances, and had collected a '*petit cadeau*' as he genteelly described it—the modest sum of sixty guineas—to present to her on the part of Mozart's English admirers. Although Mr Novello was undoubtedly kindhearted and sentimental, he was also a successful and perspicacious music publisher. His visit to Mozart's widow and old sister in Salzburg was avowedly prompted by his ardent desire to acquire if possible some unpublished manuscripts and personal relics of his idol.

Although the two elderly widows lived almost side by side in this small provincial town they rarely met. From the day that Wolfgang had fallen in love with Constanze, Nannerl had conceived an even stronger prejudice against her than Leopold. All Constanze's little presents and blandishments had not succeeded in overcoming it. In 1783 Wolfgang had taken his bride to Salzburg to introduce her to his father and sister. But the visit had not been a success. From 1820 onwards

<hr>

[1] *A Mozart Pilgrimage*, p. 85.

Constanze was living there in comfort, and when Nissen died in 1826 he left her tolerably well off. On the death of her own pompously titled husband, poor Nannerl had gone back to her native town and once again became a music teacher there. But she became blind in old age and the Novellos were deeply distressed to find her living almost in penury. She had either given away or sold most of Mozart's early manuscripts in her possession. She died in 1829, aged seventy-eight.

Chapter XIV

IMMORTALITY

MOZART 'should have died hereafter'. For had he lived, the financial security and professional success he had longed for so ardently would certainly have come to him. Within almost months of his death his works began to triumph wherever they were performed and have gone on doing so ever since.

His short life was full of ironical twists and turns of fate. But perhaps none was more ironical than the fact that Salzburg, the city he hated more than any place on earth, should so soon have become his shrine. Constanze died there in 1842, an old lady of seventy-nine. By this time she was held in respect and almost reverence by the townspeople, who at Mass would whisperingly point out Mozart's widow to visitors and admirers.

Today Salzburg remains the centre of Mozart's cult. An annual opera festival and concerts take place in his native city, when his works are performed by the world's greatest conductors, singers, and instrumentalists before an audience that flocks from every continent on earth to hear them. And then the adorers visit the house in which he was born and the home in which he lived during his years of servitude, eating out his heart in frustration and bitterness.

Apart from their performances at Salzburg, Mozart's principal operas are now given in special festival performances elsewhere and are in the regular repertoire of nearly every opera house in the world.

Gramophone records have been made over and over again of nearly all his works, and hardly a day or even an hour passes when one or another of Mozart's compositions is not on the air somewhere around our globe. Were he alive today, when adequate royalties are paid to composers, he would be one of the richest men on earth.

Like most men of genius Mozart has his legend, and this legend has frequently obscured the facts both of his life and his character. Thousands of books have been written about the man and his music. Although he himself never grew old or even middle-aged, by the time they wrote about him most of his biographers—even his wife—had outlived their own youth. Perhaps it was because they had not remembered their own youthful reactions sufficiently vividly that they so frequently adopted either a sentimental or reprobatory attitude towards their subject. To many of them he seemed either 'too rare and good for human nature's daily food' or else frivolous, irresponsible, and incompetent.

Yet there is one infallible source of information about him available to all who care to seek it—his own very considerable correspondence. This, as we know, was not meant for publication, but was strictly private, between himself, his family, and his friends. Poor Mozart might well have turned in his anonymous grave at the thought that his miserable begging-letters to Puchberg and others would be bared to posterity, were it not for the fact that even when writing them he showed himself proud and conscious of the genius which posterity's acclaim has so triumphantly confirmed. He was not an aristocrat by birth but possessed that aristocracy of character and intellect that no genealogy in itself, however exalted, can confer. Yet his letters also reveal his weaknesses in plenty—his youthful frivolity, his over-optimism (probably a trait inherited from his mother), and occasional disingenuousness; his impatience, irritability, and even tactlessness when dealing with his social superiors or musical rivals such as Clementi, for whom he felt professional contempt. He had a delightful sense of humour, but also a merciless tongue.

The self-portrait that emerges from his letters is supplemented and occasionally corrected by Leopold's. His pride in his son both as composer and performer is counter-balanced by disapproval of his weaknesses and occasional lapses as a youth and a man. Finally there are Frau Mozart's few letters to her husband during the Mannheim-Paris trip, when her son's behaviour was causing her much anxiety, probably due in great part to the good lady's fears of what his father would say to his 'goings-on'.

Many contemporary witnesses have described Mozart's personality and behaviour, some of them—mostly his rivals, of course—sneeringly and contemptuously. But those who really knew him, like Joseph Haydn, Kelly and the Storaces, all loved and respected him. And finally there is the vivid, intimate verbal portrait of him drawn by Constanze for the Novellos, when they visited her in Salzburg.

Physically Mozart was small, short, and in later years somewhat dumpy, but neatly built. His head was large, the forehead high, wide and intellectual, the nose long, rather noble. The chin was determined and even obstinate. He had a mass of fair hair, of which he was, apparently, vain; there are several references in the letters from Vienna to the early morning arrival of his hairdresser. His eyes were large and blue, and often had a vague, almost vacant expression, as if he were (as he probably was) listening to some inner melody. His hands—the hands of a great virtuoso of the piano—were exquisite, both delicate and strong. And whenever he sat down at the instrument all vagueness vanished from his expression. Lange seems admirably to have caught his appearance then, in the unfinished portrait which is said to have been his best likeness.

His voice, Constanze said, was soft and gentle, except on rare occasions, generally either in rehearsal or performance when the artists failed to fulfil his instructions precisely. This is well illustrated by a story told by Nissen: 'In Berlin, in 1789, during a performance of *The Seraglio*, in Pedrillo's aria, "Now for battle", the second violins by playing D sharp instead of D natural at the words "Only cowards are afraid", were turning a fresh and piquant progression into a mere cliché; Mozart astonished the house, and revealed his identity, by crying out "Damn it, play D natural!" ' and according to Constanze in his anger he stamped his foot so hard that the heel fell off his shoe.

He had unusual verbal facility, could improvise rhymes and doggerel on any occasion. He was convivial and loved company. His favourite game was billiards. Kelly described the fine billiard-table in his house, adding that Mozart never failed to beat him on the many occasions when he played with him.

Yet it would be a great mistake to imagine that Mozart was just a jolly, Papageno-like little man. His natural gaiety came from his mother, but Leopold's humour was wry, with a bitter tang to it, and this ironical twist also underlay many of

Wolfgang's apparently trivial jokes. After he ceased to be a prodigy—from the time of his return from Italy to Salzburg and until he left Colloredo's service in 1781—he knew years of intense bitterness and frustration. Even during his early successful years in Vienna he was not wholly happy. In the last years of his life he suffered from poverty, want, debts, and almost permanent anxiety, added to constant disappointment and a sense of failure. He was always an extrovert and did not keep his grievances to himself, but poured them out in his letters, and no doubt in his conversation. But he was also a musical genius. He transmuted all his sorrows—great or petty—into divine music, raising his own and our meaner selves as well to an altogether different spiritual level. One need only remember that dreary summer of 1788, during which he composed his three last and greatest symphonies whilst hag-ridden by sordid worries—and wrote them all down in the space of six weeks. His output was staggering and he excelled in every form he attempted.

Mozart believed in God, in himself, and in humanity. His Masonic music is filled with deep mysticism. Although he experienced the highest peaks of love and creative ecstasy, and knew, too, the blackest depths of hatred and despair, his ideal —as he wrote to Leopold—was the golden mean of the great philosophers. Both as man and composer Mozart was forever straining against his bonds. He longed to live in physical and mental freedom, in economic security, to serve no master but his inspiration. He strove to the end of his life to free himself creatively from the trammels imposed on his musical style by the conventions of his period. He died too young, worn out by overwork and struggle. But in his music—as the last movement of the 'Jupiter' symphony triumphantly proclaims—lay his immortal victory.

INDEX